Footfalls in the Silence
A Memoir

JOHN BARNIE

INDEPENDENT INNOVATIVE INTERNATIONAL

Published by Cinnamon Press,
Meirion House,
Tanygrisiau,
Blaenau Ffestiniog,
Gwynedd
LL41 3SU
www.cinnamonpress.com

The right of John Barnie to be identified as author of this work has been
asserted by him in accordance with the Copyright, Designs and Patent Act,
1988. © 2014 John Barnie. ISBN 978-1-909077-28-7

British Library Cataloguing in Publication Data. A CIP record for this book
can be obtained from the British Library.

Designed and typeset in Garamond by Cinnamon Press. Cover design by
Jan Fortune from original artwork 'Intriguing' by Zacarias Pereira Da Mata
© Zacarias Pereira Da Mata, agency: Dreamstime.com,
Cinnamon Press is represented by Inpress and by the Welsh Books Council
in Wales.
Printed in Poland
The publisher gratefully acknowledges the support of the Welsh Books
Council.

Acknowledgments

'On the Post' first appeared in *The Gobannian*.
My thanks to John Pickles for sharing his memories of the
English Department and the Shakespeare Institute at
Birmingham University, and to Helle Michelsen and Bruce
Clunies Ross for reading and commenting on the typescript.
Also to Jan Fortune of Cinnamon Press for her considerate
editing.
Frontispiece: Monica Bennett and John Barnie. The Blorenge,
circa 1960.

Contents

Folks, you wouldn't expect me to tell you everything, would you?
It's impossible to tell you everything!

Papa Charlie Jackson,
'Your Baby Ain't Sweet Like Mine'

Footfalls in the Silence

Part One

Mirrors

What do we see when we look in mirrors? Not what others see, and not just because the mirror reverses our features. Others see us through their own conception of who we are, assembled over time and perhaps from many sources. Nor do we see ourselves as we feel inside, someone we have always known yet would be hard put to define. When I look in the mirror, I see a stranger, familiar perhaps, but someone I have never spoken to, and perhaps would not want to.

Photographs are also mirrors, and moving film. There too I see the stranger. He glances up at a CCTV screen entering a supermarket, one of a crowd. There he is in a queue at the bank caught on the monitor; not at all remarkable.

I have a photograph of myself and my brother when I was about twelve and he was seven. I recognise the neighbour's garden where it was taken. My brother is sitting cross-legged under a trellis of roses and I am squatting behind him. He is wearing a shirt and tie, but it is summer and I am stripped to the waist. Above us, strung across the trellis is a large pennant that says 'BRITANNIA' in white on a dark background. I know it is a photograph of my brother and me, but I do not know, and will never know, what I felt or thought, or what else I did that day. I am looking at a mirror image of the stranger when he was young.

Memory too is a mirror. Most of an individual's past is blank. There are weeks, months, years, that have vanished, or are recalled as a sort of residue, a blur of attitudes and moods. What we call memory is composed of arbitrary snapshots, fragments of amateur footage from a film that was never made. These can relate to central events in a life though I don't think memory has any notion of centrality. Memories are not graded according to importance, they jostle one another like a sea of bobbing corks.

Once an event has lodged in the memory for whatever reason, it is developed like a photograph. Recalled years later, the image or footage is always the same. One day when I was thirteen or fourteen I walked with my friend Malcolm Elliott along the banks of the Usk. He had a small dog, perhaps a terrier, that trotted ahead of us. Suddenly the dog bounded into a patch of willow bushes. When Malcolm and I ran up, the dog came out with a dead snake in its mouth which it tossed in the grass. The snake landed on its back to reveal the primrose yellow scales on its belly. That is the irreducible core of the memory, the intense, unexpected yellow that shone in the sun like nothing I had seen. I think I must have been sorry for the needless death of the snake, but the memory is about this vivid unimaginable yellow. Perhaps Malcolm who became a biologist picked the snake up and that is when I saw its belly; perhaps the dog did not toss it in the grass. I cannot be sure, though that is how I might tell it as a story. On that day there must have been the constant purling of the river as it rushed over stones in the shallows, perhaps we saw dippers and sand martins, perhaps we only walked as far as the monument to the boy who drowned, or on to Llanwenarth. We would have talked. But all that is conjecture, the probing of the mind around the central image, the only real memory, of the snake's wonderful yellow scales.

Memory adheres to such detail and calls it truth. This or that happened to me, it is part of who I am.

But what of all the days, amounting to years, about which I remember nothing? Day by day as I move through time, or time moves through me, I think I know who I am by reference to people around me, familiar objects and places, a certain consistency perhaps in my own thoughts and feelings, but the *history* of who I am is a jumble of images among inchoate debris, images that become objectified as I recall them, or as they appear unbidden and often unwanted in the mind, so that here too I am looking at the stranger.

Here are a few such images taken at random.

I am a prefect at King Henry VIII's Grammar School and have been told by a master to watch over a class, perhaps the third form. I have never done this. It goes all right except for one boy who is mischievous, always looking at me with a sly smile to see how I will react. At last I rush out and down the corridor, get hold of a dap, bend him over a desk and give him six slaps with the sole of the shoe. I think I hit him quite hard but cannot be sure. He never loses that sly smile; he doesn't protest or cry. All the time it is as if I watch myself doing this, and in memory I watch myself watching myself. I am not angry but I appear to be. What I am watching is myself humiliate myself. I do not like power. I do not know how to deal with it.

I am in Hillerød, a town in the north of Sjælland in Denmark where I live. I am walking with someone in a street near the house but I have no memory of who it is. Suddenly there is a sparrow perched in a hedge at the level of my shoulder. It is remarkably tame. Then I see that its left eye has been damaged. The cornea is at a right angle to the eye, exactly as if it were a porthole opened on its hinge, perhaps to let in some air. It is a window onto the terrible darkness of the suffering of the bird.

I am in the Forest of Dean with my parents and my brother. I am about twelve again and he is seven. My brother and I have wandered off among the trees, perhaps playing cowboys and Indians. In the distance a band-saw begins to wail as it cuts through wood. We must be near a saw mill. What's that? my brother asks. I say it is the Banshee and it's coming to get us. My brother looks scared and I laugh and start running between the trees toward where I know our parents are. I can run faster than my brother who is terrified now and cries as he stumbles after me.

I don't like the stranger in these mirrors; I don't like a world where a tiny bird has to endure such pain.

Begin again.

I am perhaps sixteen and she is fourteen. I have been to a meeting in Park Crescent at the home of Chris Seralis, Curate of St Mary's, because I knew she would be there. Perhaps it was a Bible reading class, perhaps not. I have never been out with her, but as the meeting breaks up I offer to cycle with her to Hatherleigh Road, off the Brecon Road, where she lives. She agrees. When we get outside it is snowing and has been for some time — thick, heavy snow falling silently in the light of the street lamps. People go their different ways, wheeling bikes because the road is slippery, leaving tyre tracks and footprints in their wake. She and I wheel our bikes, too, down the Crescent. Then we stop, I cannot remember why. On our left is my grammar school, on the right St Michael's Convent School where I went until I was eleven. Before us is the Roman Catholic Church of Our Lady and St Michael on Pen-y-pound. Snow is pouring over our world in a great silence. In front of the church and to the right is a life-sized figure of

Christ on the Cross, his white body hanging patiently under a pitched wooden roof half-glimpsed through the blur of the flakes. We each hold the handlebars of our bikes and I remember that we are looking at each other, but if we said anything I do not remember. Our footprints and cycle tracks fade away behind us, before us is the white unblemished surface of the road and the hanging Christ. I experience this at the highest pitch of intensity at being alive.

Another snowscape. The Black Mountains are deep in snow shining white. I have climbed the Rholben and walk along its back toward the Sugar Loaf. The snow is a foot deep with an icy crust that sparkles in the sun. At each step the crust holds for a moment, then collapses under my weight, so my progess is up-down, up-down, up-down, my breath snorted out in spurts into the cold air. I climb the last hundred feet of the Sugar Loaf using my hands to get a purchase. Snow on the summit has been turned into a layer of cobbled ice and I am hit by the force of a North wind that snatches away my body heat. I can't stay long, but there before me are the Black Mountains and Brecon Beacons, their ridges deep in snow, still and silent, except for the wind buffeting my body, snagging on the rocks of the summit. I have a feeling I often get in the hills of a heightened sense of the *thisness* of being alive, dwarfed by the vastness, yet energised by it at the same time. Afterwards, it stays with me for days in the ordinariness of the town.

I say 'I', but I am watching this boy who may have been me once but is not and cannot be me now.

I read somewhere that total recall would drive a person mad. It would overload the carrying capacity of the brain. That is why we forget, the brain erasing vast areas of the past, schooldays that once seemed

17

interminably long, reduced to a few images, a few scenes that can be played through fast then stored for another day. Memory records experience that happened in time, it could hardly do anything else, but in memory it is time speeded up, time that fragments, leaps about without chronology. Photographs sometimes show scenes of which you have no recollection and unless they are captioned you may not know where they were taken or in which year. Then you are really in the dark. That is why old photographs on market stalls can seem so melancholy; reflections in sepia or black and white in search of the sitters, in search of their names.

Do some people have an aural memory? Mine is almost entirely visual. I can remember the sound of the school bell, a hand bell that was kept in the corridor by the main entrance of the grammar school, and was rung by one of the prefects at the end of every lesson; and the sound of a Hall or Castle Class express as it pounded through Abergavenny Monmouth Road Station when I was a trainspotter — the singing in the line, then the sight of the train as it came round the bend from the Junction, the hammering of its wheels and pistons that shook the bridge if you were standing on it, a flash of green engine and of brass, then you were enveloped in a cloud of steam and smoke, and it was gone, clattering and dwindling down the line toward Pontypool.

I can remember too the clatterclatterclatterclatter of wagons and goods vans on a frosty November evening as they were shunted at the Junction above Pen-y-val Asylum. Mostly, though, it is images I remember, which makes me suspicious of other people's recall of whole conversations. If I remember conversation it is never more than a phrase or sentence usually connected with humiliation —

Me during a cricket match against Cardiff High School : 'Owzat!'

Harold 'Acer' Sharpe, Latin master and umpire: 'Silly arse.'

Even though my memory is almost entirely visual, one thing I am often unable to recall is people's faces. I can see their bodies, remember what they were doing on a particular occasion, but when I try to look at the face it is a blur, like television news footage of the face of a suspect. I went with my first girlfriend Monica for seven years, yet were it not for three photographs, I would not be able to imagine her face. And that is the lure and deceit of photography which gives you the mirror image of a moment and allows you to see the face. With many people it is the face in the photograph I 'remember', superimposing it on the frustrating blur in the mind.

Why is memory so visual? It is a gallery of images where only an occasional footfall disturbs the silence.

Books

It is said we only remember two percent of what we read. I would say that is optimistic. I don't remember when I began to read, but from about the age of eight I read a great deal. Since my parents didn't read books and had no opinion on them I was free to read what I liked, and what I liked were the children's books of the period. I read many of Enid Blyton's Famous Five and Rachmel Crompton's Just William stories and Captain W.E. Johns' Biggles books as well as the Billy Bunter novels by Frank Richards. Slightly later, I read most of Arthur Ransome, and then John Buchan and John Masters. Yet I remember nothing of the Famous Five, or William, or Biggles, and from the Bunter books I remember only one scene when the boys jump a tramp seen acting 'suspiciously' outside the school.

What I 'remember' of Buchan's *The Thirty-Nine Steps* comes from seeing film and television adaptations later on. I remember nothing of Buchan's other novels, though when sometime in the late 1950s Penguin issued a set of ten in their distinctive orange and white covers I bought and read them all. Arthur Ransome too is a blank, except for a vague sense of young people messing about with a yacht on, was it, Lake Windermere, in, perhaps, *Swallows and Amazons*?

I must have read a hundred or more books by these authors and apart from the incident with the Greyfriars boys and the tramp, only two scenes stand out. The most vivid is from a Bulldog Drummond novel. I cannot remember the title only that it had a lurid cover of the kind Corgi paperbacks had in the

'50s. It would be considered a classic period design now.

Drummond has entered a darkened house where the man he is pursuing has laid a dastardly trap. As he mounts the stairs, cautiously, Bulldog notices that one of the steps has been booby-trapped. Step on it and it will release a weighted boomerang to sweep down and break your neck. Drummond steps over the trap. There is a gap in the narrative here in my memory, but then Drummond and this man are engaged in a deadly struggle. They crash into the bathroom where the bath has been filled with acid. (The villain had planned to dissolve Bulldog's body in it once he had been killed by the trap.) But Drummond turns the tables, lifts the man up and plunges him in the bath. The man explodes screaming to the surface, his clothes dissolving in the acid, his skin a ghastly copper colour. 'Poor devil,' Drummond thinks for a moment. Then the man rushes out of the bathroom, stumbling down the stairs to be killed by the boomerang when he treads on the step.

The other is from a John Masters novel set in India during or just after the War. Again the title has gone, but it was an orange and white Penguin. It is a warm tropical night. A man and a woman are standing by a car. She is in a silk wrap or dressing gown. Suddenly she undoes the cord and holds open the gown. Underneath it she is completely naked.

Why from all my reading at this time does the scene from Bulldog Drummond remain with me? It has something to do with the fascination of the horror, the detail of that copper-coloured skin as the doomed man scrambles out of the bath. But crucial in my mind is Bulldog's murmured 'Poor devil', as he almost but not quite regrets dropping him into the acid. For a second in this cheap thriller, Drummond,

21

the hard man's hard man, reveals a capacity for fellow feeling. There is a flicker of humanity on the page and then it is gone. Is that what soldered it onto my memory, an obscure insight into the fact that as a man it is permitted to feel sympathy?

I know very well, however, why I remember the woman and the gown. I am perhaps fifteen and sex is beginning to consume me. The scene is a revelation. It is wonderful. I had no idea a woman might do such a thing. I doubted though whether any woman in Abergavenny would do it; at least not any woman I might be likely to meet.

Great in Small Things

In his poem 'Piano' D.H. Lawrence is taken back to his childhood by a woman singing at the piano until in his mind he becomes a child again,

A child sitting under the piano, in the boom of the tingling strings
And pressing the small, poised feet of a mother who smiles as she sings.

I haven't read Lawrence's poetry for years, but those lines have always stayed with me, or more accurately, the mood evoked by them because I have never had a head for quotations. I came across it in Lawrence's *Selected Poems* in the Penguin Poets series, bought, I see, in 1960 when I was nineteen. I must have acquired it in my last year in sixth form or perhaps my first term at Birmingham University when I felt alone and unhappy.

What I like about the lines is the way in which Lawrence effortlessly sketches in the child's perspective sitting there under the piano, the juxtaposition of 'boom' and 'tingling', the detail of the mother's 'small, poised feet', the child up close to them, pressing them partly in play, partly as an expression of love for this woman who towers above him.

There is much of the poet in that child's perspective. As we grow physically we grow away, literally, from the ground-level viewpoint of our early years. As adults we look to more distant horizons, forgetting the world at our feet which the child sees so clearly because he is part of it. A poet never loses that perspective; it is fundamental to the imagination that combines experience into startling new images. Stamp collectors and bird watchers may be said to have it, to the extent that they must cultivate attention to detail, to watermarks and perforations or plumage and song, if they are to become experts. But it is different with a poet who must notice *everything* because he cannot know in advance what will be transformed into metaphor. Often it will be something trivial which is of little importance in his personal life but which the creative mind seizes on for its own ends. In the medieval poem *Cleanness*, the anonymous poet likens the fall of the multitude of angels from Heaven to flour as it is sifted through a sieve. The domestic image enacts in miniature the dreadfulness of the event — so many particles of flour cascading through the sieve, so many angels falling helplessly from Heaven. The poet did not 'think up' that simile, it entered his mind suddenly and fully formed as he wrote; a memory perhaps of watching his mother sieve flour when he was a child which he never thought he would have a use for.

Much of my early childhood was spent, like Lawrence, below the horizon of adults, manoeuvring my Dinky Toy army lorries and tanks among table legs and feet under the kitchen table, or out in my father's garden which was ablaze with flowers all summer. As the tanks laboured over the earth they would be dwarfed by forest clumps of wallflowers or golden yellow daisies I never learned the name of. The daisies in particular attracted insects, and on a level with my face, suddenly, would be a red admiral or lesser tortoiseshell, its proboscis curling and uncurling as it clambered over the packed brown stamens. Close to my eyes I could see the fine down on the abdomen, the cumbersome, slightly trembling movement of the legs, the large compound eyes, and each scale on the colourful panels of the wings as they were opened or clapped shut. There were honey bees and bumble bees, too, and hoverflies with deceptive wasp-like markings, stock-still in air, their wings a scarcely discernible blur as they inspected a flower then sped off faster than the eye could follow only to pull up short and hover again.

If I lifted a large stone there might be an ants' nest, exposed tunnels disappearing into the ground, hundreds of eggs like grains of rice, and panic, a milling about of red or black bodies humping eggs as big as themselves, seemingly without order or plan, bumping into each other, losing the egg, struggling to pick it up, until I put the stone back. Ants above all seemed hardly alive; they were automata, armoured nightmare machines that I thought nothing of killing. They got into the house, making raids on the pantry and sometimes my parents would hunt out a nest and pour boiling water on it. Ants were fair game, or so I thought then.

Everywhere, it seemed, there were things at my level, though rarely humans. During the War years and for some time afterward I spent as much time at my Aunt May's in North Street as I did at home. In spring and summer my much older cousin Cynthia, and Sheila the London refugee, would take me on walks down Upper Pentre Lane then back along Lower Pentre Lane. The walk seemed long, though in adult terms it was short. Perhaps it was long because there was so much to stop for, white, blue and yellow flowers in hedge banks; bird nests hidden in hawthorn with emerald leaves called 'bread and cheese' you could eat; pussy willows for Cynthia and Sheila to reach up and snap twigs off, as well as sticky buds from horse-chestnuts, taken home for Aunt May

25

who set them in a glass jug on the parlour table. Willow buds never came into leaf and eventually dropped off, but sticky buds opened into soft wrinkled hands. They too died at last and were thrown away. I liked to see silver bubbles of air that adhered to their twigs in the water.

Purgatory

Each year on All Souls Day the nuns of my primary school led us in prayer for the souls in Purgatory. Prayer helps release the souls so they can go to Heaven. I had a picture in my mind of the souls in a wooden enclosure packed tight like sheep in Abergavenny market. They wore long grey robes and somehow you couldn't see their faces, they were just souls, thousands upon thousands of them. I pressed my hands together, closed my eyes and prayed. One prayer could release a soul.

I didn't believe this, in fact I never believed anything I was told about religion either by the nuns or by Canon Davies at St Mary's, the Canon with beetle brows glowering at us from the pulpit in black and white robes like a disgruntled magpie. I didn't believe anything I heard during morning assembly at King Henry VIII's Grammar School either with its lessons from the Bible and hymns. Religion was something adults believed in or said they did, which you had to go along with because adults held the power.

The nuns must have believed, otherwise they wouldn't have dressed as they did in black habits that came down to their shoes, faces pinched in white head-dresses topped with a wimple, a black rosary at the waist. The nuns, you felt, were not altogether human though most of them were kind. I suppose Canon Davies believed too in his joyless way, but I doubt my headmasters at King Henry's did, the grim and feared Mr Newcombe or Colonel Edwards who, though strict, lacked the savageness of his predecessor. They had to go through the motions of morning assembly nonetheless, listening to the cycle of readings from the Bible and the same mangled hymns year after year, probably more bored than we were.

At the grammar school, Assembly was in the main hall which during the rest of the day became the fourth and fifth form classrooms divided by a partition. For Assembly the partition was folded back and the school filed in, turning left or right according to the form you were in, to stand facing each other across the width of the hall. In the middle to the left was a lectern where the headmaster stood and below him a second lectern where the lesson was read by the sixth formers in rotation. Colonel Edwards, bald and plump with round wire-rimmed glasses, looked over the head of the reader. He didn't seem to be listening, though something in him must have been.

Howard Beardsmore: And lo! Jesus spent forty days in the desért.

Colonel Edwards: Désert, boy, désert.

In the primary school there was a cabinet of natural curiosities on the stairs. It was kept locked but you could look in through its glass doors as you passed. What impressed me was an ostrich egg, massive and white, with a hole drilled at each end so you could see the shell must be a quarter of an inch thick. Sometimes one of the nuns would open the cabinet and take it out and let you hold it. There were other eggs too and a coral skeleton that looked like a tightly packed brain. I donated a centipede to the cabinet. It was about six inches long floating in formalin in a slim glass tube that had a cork stopper. It had belonged to an uncle of my mother who had been a lighthouse keeper at Alexandria in Egypt before the First World War. The centipede was amber coloured and the liquid it floated in a clear yellow.

The contents of the cabinet would have given me a perspective on religion if only I had held the key of science. But unsurprisingly the nuns never mentioned Darwin, nor did anyone in the grammar school, not even the biology mistress Myfanwy 'Fanny' Jones. So the eggs and coral and other natural objects remained curiosities without relation to one another, like the butterflies and hoverflies in my father's garden.

I did the duffer's course in 'human biology' for O-level because I needed a science, but there was never any suggestion that humans had evolved. It is possible that Mrs Jones didn't know it herself in 1954 because palaeoanthropology was still in the early stages of its development. In the same way in geography E.O. Jones taught us nothing about plate tectonics because he had never heard of it. Alfred Wegener had published *The Origin of Continents and Oceans* in German in 1929 but his theory of continental drift was dismissed by scientists until the discovery of seafloor spreading in the 1950s at a time when E.O. was still dictating from notes made at the end of the Great War. Yet looking at a Mercator's projection of the world I often noticed that Africa and South America would fit snugly together if you ignored the intervening ocean and wondered why.

The Black Mountains

It's not that I went into the mountains that often; but I was always aware of them. When I drew back my bedroom curtains in the morning there was the Sugar Loaf looming over the Deri, the Rholben and the Llanwenarth Breast that spread out from its base like the toes of a giant bird. Some thought the Sugar Loaf was an extinct volcano, but I knew from A-level geography that it was composed of Old Devonian sandstone, capped with millstone grit, and that hundreds of millions of years ago the Black Mountains had been formed on the bed of a sea. Over millions of years it became a raised plateau. Millions of years on again and the plateau had eroded to the rolling hogback hills and deep narrow valleys of my time, Y Mynydd Du in Welsh, the Black Mountains to me.

I knew this because A-level geography had a geological component, and because when I got to sixth form E.O. had retired and we had a new and energetic geography teacher, Mr Ashton, who had been an officer in the Royal Navy. Mr Ashton had a car and took us on field trips — the sixth form was small at King Henry's and there were only three or four of us studying geography. That was something extraordinary, to drive up into the Black Mountains or across Llangattock Mountain with someone who knew what the landscape *meant* and to be shown corrie lakes and the characteristic U-shaped valleys gouged by glaciers during the last Ice Age. St Mary's Vale and St David's Vale between the Deri, Rholben and Llanwenarth Breast, I now discovered, were hanging valleys, formed by tributary glaciers to the massive one that had created the Usk valley below. But even Mr Ashton had not heard of Wegener and continental drift.

I would not like to put E.O. Jones down. He was a tall, slow-moving, gentle man, and had probably had enough of teaching by the time I knew him. He never raised his voice. After serving in the First World War he had been in the Black and Tans in Ireland. I don't know how I knew this; perhaps he told us in class one day. I only found out about the Black and Tans' brutal reputation later. I doubt though whether E.O. had been involved in any atrocities.

Walking through Bailey Park on my way to King Henry's I often had to run the gauntlet of older boys from Hereford Road Primary School most of whom were bound for the secondary modern. Sight of a King Henry's uniform elicited an immediate response — 'Grammar slug! Grammar slug!' One dinner time in autumn (I always went home for midday dinner) some of the boys and I started throwing acorns at each other, from a safe distance. As I bent to pick up more ammunition I suddenly saw E.O. walking toward me. Some masters would have given me a telling off but all E.O. said was, 'Ignore them, John' in his gentle voice as he strolled past and through the big wrought iron gates at the Hereford Road end of the Park.

The Hoodoo King

Stanley and other late nineteenth-century explorers often remark on the prominence of witchdoctors among tribes of Central Africa. Witchdoctors can hunt out malefactors and have them put to death, they can discover stolen goods, make rain, put a curse on you or take a curse off, they can cure illness and discover who made you ill, because nothing is accidental or as it seems. The explorers, with European civilization behind them, naturally believed none of this, but had they turned their sceptical eye on their own faith, Christianity, they would have seen the biggest witchdoctor of them all. Jesus can raise the dead, heal the sick, give eyesight to the blind, walk on water, turn five loaves of bread and two fishes into a meal for five thousand, turn water into fine wine, magic his own body away from a rocky tomb.

Jesus of course had a good teacher in his father Yahweh who among other feats parted the Red Sea to save Moses and the children of Israel from Pharaoh's army. The mechanism whereby he did this is not entirely convincing — according to Exodus he caused 'a strong east wind' to blow all night which parted the waves and dried the seabed; and when he removes the wheels of the Egyptians' chariots halfway across, the vandalism of juvenile delinquents comes to mind.

My Bible had an illustration. It showed the Red Sea parted in two towering blue-green glassy walls. Below were the tiny figures of the Egyptians galloping along the seabed and beyond on the farther shore Moses and the Israelites turning back to look. At any moment Yahweh will give the sign, the walls will collapse, and the Red Sea be strewn with the bodies of men and horses, the splintered wreckage of chariots.

Relocate these stories to a nineteenth-century village on the Congo and it can be seen at once how outlandish and unbelievable they are. Yahweh was a god of course rather than a witchdoctor and Jesus the son of a god, but Jesus was also flesh and blood. No European explorer encountering a Congo witchdoctor who claimed he could walk on water would have believed him, any more than he would have believed a witchdoctor who claimed to cure malarial fever by waving a fetish bag over the afflicted. The explorer would suspect an imposter or seek a rational explanation for a supposedly magical cure. If he himself succumbed to fever it was not a fetish he reached for but a bottle of quinine. For these men were overwhelmingly drawn from military, scientific or medical backgrounds; they dealt with hard facts in a rational, material world.

'The more experience and insight I obtain into human nature,' Stanley mused in *In Darkest Africa*, 'the more convinced do I become that the greater portion of a man is purely animal.' Stanley had seen enough of humanity to know, yet even he left the door ajar — only 'the *greater portion* of a man is purely animal'. In the accounts of his expeditions, Stanley inserts a profession of Christianity now and then, when he can remember, but it is a shallow late nineteenth-century piety that rings hollow when compared with his life as a man of action. It is impossible to know what he really believed, and perhaps he did not know himself, or perhaps part of him was reluctant to state publicly what he knew, so he used 'faith' like mock Tudor panelling that hides a concrete wall.

My parents were born either side of Stanley's death in 1904, my father in 1902, my mother in 1908. They were Stanley's children in that they were brought up in the world he had helped to make and uncritically accepted its values. My mother in particular might have been a member of the League of Empire Loyalists in the 1950s. To her Great Britain simply meant Britain was Great, the centre of the most powerful and benevolent empire the world had ever seen; it was the world's manufactory too, with Birmingham and the Black Country, where she had relatives, at its hub.

Thomas Heazle Parke's *My Personal Experiences in Equatorial Africa as Medical Officer of the Emin Pasha Relief Expedition*, published in 1891, has two vignettes by Stanley's artist wife Dorothy Stanley. On the front cover in gold on an olive green background is an outline map of Africa showing the Congo, the Nile, the 'Mountains of the Moon' and Lake Victoria. Dorothy Stanley might have based it on the large oilcloth maps that would have hung in schools in late Victorian times and which still existed in my schools in the 1940s and early 1950s. Beneath it, looking up, are two naked boys, one white, one black. The white boy has his arm round the waist of the black boy, protectively you, might say, but also with a certain proprietorial air. He is pointing up to the River Congo, showing the black boy where he lives. On the title page two naked black boys are sitting on the ground. One holds a pot of paint while the other, concentrating hard, paints his friend white. The boy being painted has a broad smile.

My parents were brought up on such images of Empire and would have seen nothing odd in them. In the 1950s my mother still referred to a certain dark brown as 'nigger brown'. To her it was simply a colour designation. When in the early 1960s an Abergavenny friend of mine and his American wife adopted a black child and my father patted his 'wool' neither my father nor my mother could understand why the parents were deeply offended. What had he done?

This wasn't racism in any simple overt sense, but a residue, an undertow, from the world of Empire in which they had grown up and which they never questioned. Part of this residue was Christianity, more specifically Church of England piety of the kind practised in Abergavenny in my mother's childhood. The Church went with the Union Jack and Empire, to be seen in its most literal manifestation in cathedrals where threadbare regimental flags from nineteenth-century campaigns hung in the gloom of the aisles.

By the 1950s all this was sham. There was no Empire and the 'Sea of Faith' that Matthew Arnold had seen ebbing away in 'Dover Beach' as far back as 1867 had left St Mary's Church high and dry with its dwindling congregation of the aged.

This was the debris I had to climb out from under without really knowing how to do it, though there were signposts in the books I began to read and in the natural world of the Usk and the Black Mountains. It seems strange now, but in sixth form a group of us who were atheists in embryo argued passionately about original sin, predestination versus free will, the status of miracles, transubstantiation, and the resurrection. In the process we learned without realising it how to manipulate the merciless weapons of logic. Partly because she would not let me go my own way but forced me to be confirmed against my will, and partly because I had the zeal of a convert, I applied the same techniques to my arguments with my mother. In retrospect this was unfair. What passed for Christianity in her eyes was a given on which she had never reflected. Consequently she fell back on 'because it is' or 'because the Bible says so', an impregnable last line of defence which angered me. And so we quarrelled.

At the Darwin bicentenary festival in Cambridge in 2009 Daniel Dennett among others argued that science was in direct conflict with religion, *pace* attempts to find a rapprochement between them, and that Christianity should be vigorously opposed. There was general agreement, but one scientist raised an objection. He lived in Harlem, he said, where many African-American women raised their children and sometimes their grandchildren alone. They were sustained through a lifetime of hardship by their faith. What right, he asked, did anyone have to take that from them. Dennett had earlier introduced himself from the floor as one of the Four Horsemen of the Apocalypse as far as Christianity was concerned, but even he agreed that no one had that right. The argument rather is with Christian apologists, with fundamentalist proponents of 'Intelligent Design', and with liberal theologians who spin webs of plausible argument from false premises.

This is one reason I like gospel music, especially the recordings of the great a capella quartets of the 1940s and '50s, for although they are of course rooted in Christianity, many are more nearly concerned with what it is to be human in the face of suffering and loss; they are poetic expressions that an atheist can respond to in his own way as much as a Christian.

In the 1950s, however, I did not have that perspective, and because my mother still believed she could control me as she had done when I was a child,

I fought back with all the weapons I could find, and was cruel in the process.

Down by the Riverside

Seen from the brow of the Deri, the Usk is a grey or silver thread glimpsed among fields and trees until it disappears in distant haze toward Newport where it becomes tidal, its brown water flowing between sullen mud banks, hemmed in by terraced housing.

Looking down from the Deri I can see the stretch of the river I know best from Abergavenny to Llanwenarth. I know the reaches of deep water flowing between banks of red earth where sand martins nest. There you can see large trout rising to the surface with open mouths before fading back into the brown water. They jump too for flies, but you rarely see this, always turning to the sound of the splash, watching concentric rings dissolve in the steady flow of the river.

I know the shallows where the Usk suddenly ravels out over smooth stones, sunlight fractured and scattered across rippling water. The deep pools are silent, but here it is as if sound is fractured too, a glass-like clattering, out of which may come the shrill cry of a common sandpiper as it flies low and fast upstream. You have to watch keenly in order to catch the white bib of a dipper or a kingfisher sitting intently on the stump of a post out there in the stream.

The shallows are best because I can wade out enclosed by light and sound, almost part of the river, water up to my ankles, feet feeling across cobbles slimy with algae. Turning stones over I may expose a loach or bullhead, its mottled khaki the perfect camouflage. I hold my net downstream and if I'm lucky the fish will spurt forward and I can haul it up and empty it into my jam jar with its handle of string.

I have an old glass battery case with thick bluish-green glass my father gave me as a fish tank. It will be home for the bullhead or loach as it winnows down through the column of water to the stones and sand. There are one or two sticklebacks too that I caught in Llanwenarth pond, whirring their fins noiselessly like fantastical Jules Vernes submarines. I would like to have a proper fish tank like Malcolm Elliott who keeps tropical fish in his parents' tiny living room, but my father, the improviser, says the battery tank will do.

Although I do not realise it the river is my first introduction to poetry, not words on a page but living poetry that I can see, hear and touch, and which I will always be in search of later in life. It is why poems like 'Fern Hill' and 'Poem on His Birthday' meant so much to me when I first read Dylan Thomas in sixth form, capturing as they do the sense of being enveloped by nature as a child and the shadow of exile in the adult world. This is Wordsworthian, I know, and not very fashionable.

During the same Darwin bicentenary festival in Cambridge, David Attenborough gave a speech in which he described how he became passionate about nature as a boy, collecting birds' eggs, handling small animals, picking wild flowers while he roamed the countryside at will. In his memoir, *Naturalist*, Edward O. Wilson describes the same experience in the somewhat wilder countryside of Florida and Alabama. For him, 'Hands-on experience at the critical time, not systematic knowledge, is what counts in the making of a naturalist. Better to be an untutored savage for a while, not to know the names or anatomical detail. Better to spend long stretches of

time just searching and dreaming.' R.S. Thomas knew
this too. In 'Farm Boy', a village boy's head

is stuffed
With all the nests he knows, his pockets with flowers,
Snail-shells and bits of glass, the fruit of hours
Spent in the fields by thorn and thistle tuft.

In his speech David Attenborough lamented the
fact that, for perfectly valid reasons, nature today is
hedged in by laws against egg collecting, picking wild
flowers, netting river fish for your tank (bullheads are
now an endangered species), in such a way that the
kind of boyhood he had is no longer possible. He
wondered what this might mean for a generation of
biologists brought up without that intense closeness
to nature.

I did not become a naturalist but my intimacy
with the river was to turn into a lost paradise when I
had to leave Abergavenny to go to university in
Birmingham, a paradise which later again made me a
writer, or at any rate made me the kind of writer I
am.

Often on summer evenings a gang of us would
go to Bailey Park to play cricket or throw a tennis ball
around. Sometimes, though, we would go to the
castle meadows and play there in a field of buttercups
with grazing cows and the great bulwark of the
Blorenge looming over us. As the sun set, the
mountain's black summit became razor-sharp, the sky
above turquoise shot with pink, with ribs of white
cloud like sand on the beach as the tide goes out. We
would play almost until it got dark, the sound of the
river a half-acknowledged presence. Then we
collected the stumps, bat and ball, Venus a bright
prickling light over the Blorenge, as we walked slowly

past the castle, down by the Angel Hotel, up Monk Street and Hereford Road past the closed gates of Bailey Park, and home.

King Henry VIII"s
Grammar School

As my time at the primary school came to an end I was coached in the 11-plus exam by Sister Mary Joseph who took the top class, and by my mother who bought past exam papers from Smith's and sat by me while I worked through them one by one.

'Fill in the blanks: "As black as —", "As green as —".' That was easy.

But mathematics was impossible. My mother and I went through paper after paper until brackets, plus and minus signs, square roots, triangles and circles became a misery for me. Yet somehow I tricked the examiners; I passed without understanding even the most basic principles of algebra and geometry. Because of this, in 1952, instead of walking along Park Avenue and Skirrid Road then turning right to the nuns' school, I turned left and entered the back gate of King Henry VIII's Grammar School on Peny-y-val Road.

In 1952 there were 9 members of staff, including the headmaster, and 180 pupils. Later in the '50s staff numbers rose to 11. There were two women, Mrs Jones, Biology, and the School Secretary.

You went to school because you had to. That first morning I walked up the long dark corridor to the first form room with a lot of jostling, gesticulating, shouting boys who all seemed to know each other. Being the only boy from St Michael's I knew no one and sat at the front trying not to be noticed. But one boy did notice and started to wrench my shoes off. I should have kicked him but I was unprepared and did nothing, on the edge of tears. Then another boy who knew this boy came up and made him stop. That was Malcolm Elliott who became one of my best friends at King Henry's. The other boy, P— J—, took pleasure in humiliating people as I found out more than once. He was a good musician and later in the '50s we formed a skiffle group together, but I never trusted him and when I think of those first hours of my first morning in school, I hate him still.

I do not want to say much about the grammar school except that I am glad I went there, rather than to the comprehensive which replaced it in the early 1960s with its impersonal buildings and 1200 students. (When did schoolchildren stop being 'pupils' and become 'students'; around the time of the formation of comprehensives, perhaps?)

Discipline at King Henry's was strict but fair. If you went out of line and were caught, you were punished, either with detention or in extreme cases with a caning from the Head. That was very rare though and I cannot remember an example. Most subjects were taught adequately to the O-level syllabus, though probably not more than that. Physics and chemistry were mysteries that never opened to me and I was glad to drop them when it came to making choices in fourth form. Maths O-level was supposed to be compulsory but I was such a hopeless case that it was decided not to put my name forward for the exam. Later in sixth form when contemplating a university this left me with a problem as most universities demanded O-level maths. Luckily for me Birmingham among a few others only demanded a science and I had human biology.

Day in day out for five years I did the work, suffered rugby and somewhat less so, cricket, went on the annual cross country run along the lower slopes of the Deri, never got chosen to compete on sports day, and only got into trouble once. In 1957 I gained seven O-levels, enough to get me into sixth form. There for the first time I felt a purpose because in fifth form I had come under the influence of Wyn Binding.

Wyn had been in minesweepers during the War stationed in the Red Sea and on being demobbed took advantage of the educational opportunities open to ex-servicemen by going to study English at Aberystwyth. He was from the Valleys and for reasons I forget had been brought up by his grandparents. Wyn was a forceful man who didn't tolerate disruption in class. It was common to see a piece of chalk whizz across the room if he turned from the board and saw someone talking or fooling about; or for one of us to get a clip on the head with the hard back of the board rubber. I know that some in my class resented him and perhaps even hated him, but his enthusiasm was catching and most of us looked forward to his lessons as the high point of the day. I doubt anyone else could have made O-level English Language interesting with its endless analysis of the parts of the sentence.

But Wyn was deeply committed to literature and this is what attracted me to him. It was typical of him that he found me in Smith's one day looking through their small collection of paperbacks and wondering whether to buy another John Masters. He came over and looked at the orange and white Penguin I had in my hand. 'Yes, he's good, isn't he, but have you tried this,' and he plucked out E.M. Forster's *A Passage to India* also in a Penguin. Because it was Wyn, I bought it. It was a turning point. I didn't read Masters anymore.

The grammar school being so small, I was the only boy in my year studying A-level English and there were not more than two or three in the year above me. When the two years were studying the same books, Wyn held tutorials in the school library, but when in my second year there were books on the syllabus which I alone was studying, he held a one-to-one tutorial with me, usually in the staff room.

Wyn had no 'theory' of literature though he had been influenced by the close reading techniques of the New Criticism which he put to use as we went through *Antony and Cleopatra*, *The Clerk's Tale* or *Great Expectations*. Theory, it seems to me, denies the spirit in which poets and novelists write, creating a desert where there should be a forest. In the late 1950s of course I didn't know this because I didn't know there were such things as competing theories of literature. What Wyn taught me was how to develop my senses as I read. He would do this by taking a poem, perhaps, and showing how a metaphor or symbol subsumed multiple layers of meaning within one radiant image. Or he would point to a line break and show how delicately poised a sentence was across the break, or how rhyme in a sonnet acted as a pattern in the weave of meaning.

Wyn made the technicalities of poetry come alive in this way so that you began to understand the craft of what you were reading. But above all, what you got from Wyn was the conviction that literature is important and that it says something to you, here, now, not merely about life in general but about your life too. If literature doesn't touch you, we learned, it is not worth reading. And he would illustrate this in all kinds of ways. We boys were having trouble with *The Clerk's Tale* of Patient Grisilde. We didn't think it reasonable that she should be tested in such cruel ways by her husband and meekly accept it. Wyn must have been thinking about this, because one day he came into the library with a newspaper cutting of a medieval painting of, I think, the Madonna, with her head bowed in patient suffering. That, Wyn said, is what lies at the heart of the story. He didn't convince us that time but later at university when I was studying Middle English poetry I began to understand.

At other times he would seize on a homely example to illustrate an author's fine attention to detail. There is a scene in *Great Expectations* where Pip watches Mrs Gargery cutting a piece of bread and butter. She smears butter on the bread, carefully wiping off any excess, then holding the loaf close to her chest cuts off the buttered round. That's exactly how my grandmother did it, Wyn told me. You are careful with the butter because butter is expensive and you hold the loaf like that and cut with the breadknife slowly toward you. Dickens got that exactly right. And he had. Once Wyn had pointed it out, I noticed how the mothers of some of my friends cut bread in exactly the same way.

Wyn encouraged debate, though vigorous argument might be a better term for it. He expressed his own critical opinions with an emotional force and always argued to win, and since he was our idol, this rapidly became the norm for us too. So discussion in the library was often animated. Wyn would always listen to what you said, but he was merciless if he knew you were bluffing. Dryden's 'Absalom and Achitophel' was one of the set texts. I didn't like it much and thought I'd score a point by saying I preferred Pope. Wyn told me to read some Pope after which I could come back and have an intelligent discussion, but until then I had better shut up. I was humiliated, but I knew he was right. It was another kind of lesson — always marshal your evidence; don't pretend to speak about things of which you know nothing.

Strangely, since none of us came from homes with books, I don't remember him ever encouraging us to use the public library. I had always bought books from Smith's and after I visited Wyn's house in Llanellen and saw how his living room was lined with books I knew that the thing to do was to collect them and build a library of your own. I used the university library as a student but that has been my view of books ever since.

Most of the other teachers taught strictly to the curriculum but Wyn was always branching out, enthusing about something he had just read, recommending new authors. In this way I began reading Dylan Thomas and R.S. Thomas, Salinger's *Catcher in the Rye*, Wilfred Owen, Gerard Manley Hopkins, Arthur Miller's *Death of a Salesman*, D.H. Lawrence's poems and *Sons and Lovers*, all tumbling over each other. I still think this is the way to start reading and in the end the only kind of reading that is worthwhile — following up authors, devouring them, then on to the next, reading what you *need* to read at the time.

So when I was eighteen or nineteen I read most of Lawrence, living for a while in a world where black flames of passion lapped the thighs. Today, apart from some of the poetry, I find Lawrence unreadable; but then his novels mirrored the sexual intensity of my teenage years when I was courting Monica Bennett, the girl with the bicycle in the snow that evening on Park Crescent. Lawrence was the truth for me then.

By the standards of Abergavenny in the 1950s, Wyn was unconventional. On the first day of term after the summer holidays when I was in fourth or fifth form a rumour ran from class to class — *Have you seen Basher, he's grown a beard.* I don't think we believed it until he barged into the classroom in his usual energetic manner with a rufous beard making him look a little like the sailor on packets of Player's Navy Cut. He acted as if nothing was unusual and so did we, but none of us had seen a man with a beard before, and I have often wondered how he squared it with the Head, Colonel Edwards. In sixth form I grew sideboards as long as I dared — just this side of Teddy Boy defiance. They were frequently eyed by the Colonel, though he only commented on them once. I was a postgraduate in the mid 1960s before I grew a beard in imitation of Wyn. By then, however, beards were not uncommon among contemporaries. It was a badge of rebellion against the restricting norms of society or so we thought.

Wyn was unconventional in other ways too. At the time when I was reading Lawrence I was also wrapped up in *The Catcher in the Rye*. Holden's prowling exposure of American bourgeois 'phoneyness' played out my own resistance to the staid small-town world of Abergavenny, but on a more exotic stage and with undertones of impending tragedy. That suited me perfectly, so I was shocked one day when Wyn said casually that Holden Caulfield was a repressed homosexual who struggled against his sexuality. Homosexuality was not mentioned in the petit bourgeois world of my parents, or if it was, it was only among the men, who would sometimes refer to the Coliseum cinema scandal in the 1940s when the manager committed suicide. Perhaps Wyn's directness was a result of his Valleys upbringing or an expression of his commitment to truth as he saw it.

We boys were consumed by our awakening sexual desire, though we almost never talked about it, partly because it was another taboo subject but also because we were so ignorant. In human biology in fifth form Mrs Jones had drawn diagrams of limp penises and clinical wombs in white chalk on the board but they didn't enlighten us, nor did her comment that women didn't like sex much because it hurt. Could that be true? But in sixth form Wyn elucidated the sultry sexuality of *Antony and Cleopatra* with brio. When Enobarbus says

If we should serve with horse and mares together,
The horse were merely lost; the mares would bear
A soldier and his horse...

I don't think any of us understood what it meant. Perhaps sensing this, Wyn went into a digression on a woman feeling the weight of her lover's body on top of her, adding that he hoped it wasn't something we had experienced yet. He needn't have worried. Perhaps serving in the Royal Navy in the War had something to do with his forthrightness as well.

On the Post

Christmas week, 1957, I got my first job, as a temporary postman. It was part of what was to be an annual event until I graduated, especially attractive when I was at King Henry's because it meant breaking up for the Christmas holidays a week early *and* earning some money. Usually, as I recall, only sixth formers were allowed to apply for the prized week off, but that year there must have been an unusual demand for temporaries, and a few of us fifth formers were allowed to apply as well.

No doubt because of my age, I was made a 'telegram boy' and was given a leather pouch with a strap to go crosswise over my shoulder and a heavy old Post Office bike. In between telegrams I was detailed to trundle a flatbed trolley loaded with mail from the Post Office in Frogmore Street up to the Drill Hall in Baker Street which was being used as an over-spill sorting office. That was my introduction to the coarse, tangy smell of jute mailbags which I've ever since associated with Christmas. Today mailbags are made from an odourless grey plastic weave without resonance.

Many telegrams were local within the town and I would be back on the trolley within ten minutes, but a few were what might be considered long-distance and these I enjoyed the most. One was to a farm on the slopes of the Big Skirrid. I got instructions as to where it was from the postman who worked the round, and off I went pedalling up the Ross Road. When I got to the foot of the Skirrid, however, the map in my head didn't correspond to features on the ground. I could see a farm above me, but there didn't seem to be any lane or track up to it, so I left the bike in a ditch and forced a way across frost-covered fields until I found myself in a muddy farmyard. Luckily for me it was the right farm and after putting the telegram in the hands of the farmer's wife I made a stumbling way down the frozen track she pointed out to me and eventually retrieved the bike. I freewheeled back to town, my face numbed with cold, as lights came on and dusk fell. There were no more telegrams that day.

The other 'long distance' delivery I remember was to Triley Court on the Old Hereford Road. The Court was still a private residence and I parked my bike at the entrance to the drive, walking slowly up to the imposing redbrick façade and the stone-framed doorway that was more than a little daunting. I rang the bell and what followed seems in my memory to be fixed as in a tableau. The door opened slowly and there stood a sombre grey-haired man in a very formal suit. Some way behind him in the hall was an old woman in a long old-fashioned dress staring in my direction, as if arrested by this unusual event of someone ringing at the door. The man asked me what I wanted and I gave him the telegram. He took it without a word and closed the door. Cycling there I had hoped I might get a tip, as I had from several people in the town. There was no tip, but I got something much better, the briefest glimpse into a world I had no idea existed a couple of miles from Abergavenny. I never found out whether the man at the door was the butler or the owner, or who the lady was, but I knew instinctively they belonged to a world that had outlived itself, and that the tableau effect they left on my mind was symptomatic of that — as if they had been automata, brought to life by the ringing at the door.

The following year I was given my own round which consisted of the Hereford Road from Lion Street up to the shop on the corner of Park Crescent, and all the side streets to the right — St Mary's Road, Priory Road, Oxford Street, Alexandra Road, Albert Road and Richmond Road. During Christmas week the regular postmen did the sorting for the round by street, after which letters and packets were handed to the temporary who arranged them in the best order for delivery, though of course you only knew this after you had done the round a few times. On the first morning out, I finished in about an hour and a half, and got back to the Post Office by 10.00. My postman was sitting at a sorting desk chucking letters into pigeonholes for the second delivery. He looked up.

'What are you doing here?'

'I've finished.'

'Bloody hell! You live on Hereford Road, don't you? Go home and have a cup of tea and don't come back till half-eleven.'

I hadn't realised a round was calculated to take x amount of time and that by finishing early I was undermining established procedure. From then on, when I'd reached the top of Richmond Road, I went back to the house for an hour, turning up 'on time' at the sorting office.

As I was a stamp collector, one of the pleasures of delivering mail was fishing an envelope out of the bag that had exotic stamps. 'British Empire' was my speciality, and a house on Alexandra Road was particularly intriguing. Two spinster sisters lived there and they must have had a network of relatives or friends across the globe, because on almost every round there would be letters for them from Canada, South Africa, Australia, New Zealand. These were written on flimsy airmail paper tucked inside blue, light-weight envelopes of the kind you could buy at Smith's — if you had anyone abroad to write to, that is. Some envelopes were bulky and must have contained many sheets of paper. Since no one in my family wrote letters, it was a puzzle what the sisters' correspondents could have to say at such length. But a last look at the stamps, and the letters were flicked through the letterbox to fall with a plop in the hall.

The sisters' house was Edwardian with a good letterbox from a postman's point of view because it was broad, the flap didn't have a spring, and it opened inwards. Most letterboxes were like that on my round, unlike the ones today that are designed with heat efficiency in mind rather than the convenience of someone actually trying to deliver something. So the modern letterbox flap opens outwards or has a strong spring, often combined with a stiff-bristled draught excluder. This makes life difficult for the postman who has to negotiate lifting the flap with a handful of mail in one hand while trying to push an envelope past the draught excluder with the other.

Only one house was like that on my round, a bungalow also on Alexandra Road, that had a glass panelled door with the letterbox at the bottom of the wooden frame. With a bulky mailbag blocking your view, it meant you had to kneel down and peer over the bag to locate the letterbox. The annoyance of this was compounded the first time I delivered there by a rush of snarling grey the other side of the frosted glass as a lapdog ran up to bite my fingers. I just got them back out of the letterbox in time. I had my revenge though. From then on, I jiggled the letters back and forth in the letterbox until they were snatched out of my grasp. I walked down the path to the sounds of snarling and the rending of paper the other side of the door.

I shouldn't think any postman likes dogs. With a full mailbag in front of you it is difficult to anticipate what a dog is going to do as it bounds toward you barking or growling, and sometimes an owner following saying 'Oh he won't hurt you, he's quite friendly.' Personally I wasn't going to take the chance. One house had a Beware of the Dog sign on the gate and usually the dog in question standing behind it, baring its fangs. Sometimes I took the letters back to the sorting office and tried again next day. If the dog happened to be outside again, I put them through next door's box and hoped they'd be passed on.

One of the pleasures of Christmas week was the sense of camaraderie — the warm light and the tangy smell of mailbags as you came into the sorting office out of the dark winter morning; the bustle as parcels were flung with unerring accuracy into mailbags held open on iron frames with their different destinations, or letters docketed with a flick of the wrist into the appropriate pigeonhole. There was pleasure too in sorting the round by street and house name or number, collecting them in convenient handfuls and securing them with rubber bands — Christmas cards, letters, bills; and small packets, and registered letters that you had to keep separate and remember when you came to the appropriate street; the rattatat on knockers or the hollow ringing of a bell in the hallway, and someone scurrying to the door to open it and peer out. 'Oh thank you — Merry Christmas!'

Putting on the Post Office armband each morning, struggling to get under the shoulder strap of the bulging postbag, walking up Frogmore Street and down Lion Street to the start of the round as the town eased itself into a new day, gave an intense sense of being alive, of feeling your way into another world, apart from school and the familiar world of home.

When did the hiring of temporaries start, I wonder, and when did it end? My impression is there are no temporary Christmas postmen now; or at least there don't seem to be any in Aberystwyth where I live. No doubt this is a function of the fall in the volume of post due to e-mail, but also to successive Thatcherite governments who have destroyed the Royal Mail's hated monopoly and with it the viability of the service.

Most of the post delivered to our house today is junk mail with a sprinkling of bills. In the interests of efficiency, stamps have largely disappeared, replaced by franking machines, TNT printed envelopes, the one-size-fits-all stick-on labels issued at post offices. Sorting offices too have been 'rationalised' out of existence. Abergavenny's mail is sorted in Newport, Aberystwyth's in Shrewsbury. What gets lost in all this is the sense of the local, of belonging, the intricate threads of contact that bind a community together, which all of us who worked on the Christmas post experienced at first hand.

Saint Mary's Vale

Perhaps I first went to Saint Mary's Vale, the hanging valley between the Rholben and Llanwenarth Breast, with my father when I was a child. Every year in autumn he would bundle sacks and a spade into the boot of our Standard 12 and we would drive up to the Vale, bumping and splashing across the ford where Nant Iago crosses the track and then down into the narrow U-shaped valley. No matter how sunny the day, we would be plunged into sombre shadow from the beech wood on the left and the mountain oaks that came down the Rholben to the stream on the right. To me it was one of the most beautiful places on Earth (what little of the Earth I'd seen, which then didn't extend much beyond Monmouth and Brecon). I loved the silence of it, accentuated by the splashing of the stream and perhaps a light wind in the canopy above. The large smooth boles of the beech trees retreated up the slope of the Llanwenarth Breast like pillars, the arches and spandrels of branches creating a leafy vault.

But we were here on business. Half way along, before the track made a dog-leg turn to the left up out of the Vale, my father stopped the car and got out the sacks and spade. While I held the bags open he shovelled leaf mould in until each was full. It was not the newly fallen leaves' umber brown that he was after, but the black shiny wet decaying leaf fragments that lay beneath. The track itself was deep in this litter with sunken grooves made by the postman's van and a few other visitors like my father. It was the best fertiliser you could get, he would say, though he said that about chicken manure as well, and horse dung which he'd go out and collect with a bucket and shovel when a horse left a steaming pile in Priory Road.

Perhaps my father responded to the beauty of the Vale but he never said anything that I recall. Having only ever lived in Monmouth and Abergavenny it may be he took such places for granted. It was all new to me, however, and in a strange way remained so, no matter how many times I went there.

In winter the Vale was very different. In cold weather, icicles hung from the banks of the stream and from protruding stones, the ice formed piecemeal by the splashing of the water. The stream itself was clear but black-looking. The leaf mould on the track had turned from squelchy mush to icy crispness, or to the hardness of iron in the vehicle ruts. If it had snowed, the branches of the trees were coated with powdery white; fronds of dead bracken broke the blinding white of the slopes. It was the snow coming right down to the banks of Nant Iago that made the water seem so black by contrast. Everything was still, the trees rigid sentinels, as if the world was dead but watching as you crunched over snow and dead leaves, harbouring your warmth in the dry air.

Later, when I read *Sir Gawain and the Green Knight* at university, the Vale in winter seemed just the place for the green chapel. I could see the Green Knight grinding his axe on the slope of the Rholben, then bounding down and leaping across Nant Iago for his final encounter with Sir Gawain.

In spring it was otherwise. The Vale had a green radiance from sunlight penetrating the soft leaves of oak and beech; the stream was soft, too, rippling over stones, new growth of fern and grass overhanging its banks. The birds began to return — willow warblers and chiffchaffs, wheatears and tree pipits, and occasionally a redstart or a green woodpecker, and on the horizon a raven that had never left, the bird of the moorland winter, an appropriate companion for the Green Knight.

At the end of the summer term in 1958 a group of us sixth formers decided to hold a party in the Vale and camp overnight. We loaded tents and sleeping bags and bottles of cider onto bikes and trudged with them up to a flat promontory of mountain grass that had somehow been carved out of the slope of the Rholben forty feet above the stream. With tents pitched and the sun going down over the Llanwenarth Breast, we gathered dead branches from under the oaks and fried sausages in an old frying pan. I don't suppose I drank much cider, if any, alcohol was distasteful to me then; but it was a new experience, sitting there in the growing dark, our faces glowing and shadowy as flames flickered in the fire.

At night Nant Iago clattered below over its stones. Looking out across the Vale to the Llanwenarth Breast I could see one tree towering over the others on the wooded slope. It stood out alone and silent, as if watching us under the harsh glitter of the stars.

The following year, sixth formers at the Girls' High School in Harold Road decided to copy us and went off to camp in Saint David's Vale between the Rholben and the Deri. One or two of the older boys took bottles of cider and walked across the Rholben to join them, stumbling back down to our camp after the rest of us had gone to bed. Nothing would have gone on, it was just a piece of bravado. I fell asleep to the sound of the stream and the intense wakeful stillness of the hills at night.

Home

'Home'. When you say a word slowly it can seem suddenly strange. 'Home'. Is that really how you spell it? And what does it mean? 'Hoam'. 'Hohm'.

Home for me was Elmsgrove, a two storey house built in about 1910 on the corner of Hereford Road and Priory Road and almost unchanged when I was a child. It was built of sandstone quarried on the Deri, with yellow brick surrounds to the windows. On the Priory Road side was a lean-to conservatory with red and blue glass panes in the doors and tiers of wooden shelving painted white reaching up to the sloping glass roof. At the bottom of the garden was a redbrick stable, (it still had a manger for hay), which my father used as a garage. Elmsgrove had a dining room, a front room, four bedrooms, a bathroom, two toilets, a wash house, a coal house, a kitchen, and a pantry. The pantry had a thick slab of slate running from wall to wall that was always cold and had been used to store food in the days before fridges. In the kitchen above the door to the hallway was a panel with four numbers, 1, 2, 3, 4. If you pressed a button in any of the downstairs rooms or the bedrooms on the first floor, one of these numbers would jiggle and a bell would sound summoning the maid, though when I lived there the days of maids had gone. It was bigger than the houses of any of my friends. Malcolm Elliott's had a street door that gave onto a small living room behind which was a tiny kitchen and then a concreted backyard with a shed attached to an aviary where Mr Elliott bred canaries. Malcolm would take me out sometimes to see the young in the nests. I suppose they had two bedrooms upstairs, and perhaps a bathroom.

I didn't question Elmsgrove. That's where I lived, where I ate and slept, where I was often happy and sometimes afraid. It was where my mother returned to from the shop at 12.00, to cook dinner for me, my brother, my father and herself. At 1.25 when the hooter went at Sergeant's the Printer's, it was time for me to walk back to school.

'My home ain't here', sang the old bluesmen and gospel quartets. My father died in 1981, my mother in 1990. My brother hung on in the house for several years, the conservatory rotting and collapsing until it had to be removed. Subsidence undermined one corner of the house; the floorboards rotted in the loft of the stables and a crack zigzagged through the bricks above the double doors. Elmsgrove was sold and turned into flats and I pass it by now and feel nothing. The child who lived there who was me and not-me has vanished along with sunlight in the garden, the stands of yellow daisies, the shadow of the huge mountain ash telling the time as it moved across the lawn on a summer afternoon. The tree itself has gone, its branches lopped until it was no more than a bare trunk that stood decaying in the back garden. At last it fell over, was cut into segments and carted away.

Writers

It never occurred to me you might know a writer. Most writers were dead and in the unlikely event of one being alive he or she lived a long way away. A lot of writers lived in London, and London might as well have been Vienna or Prague for all the likelihood of going there. (I did go once, briefly, with my mother to see the street decorations after the Coronation in 1953. The highlight was bumping into Mrs Jones, the mother of my classmate John Jones, on one of the main streets. They lived in St Mary's Road. That was something real and knowable you could anchor yourself to.)

Writers never wrote about Abergavenny or the Usk or the Black Mountains. These were places where you lived, but books were about other places like the mining villages of Nottinghamshire, the middle class world of the Home Counties, Imperial India, or the trenches.

I didn't know then that David Jones had lived for a while at Llanthony and had painted the hills there — people didn't paint, except Huw Davies, Art, at King Henry's, who I saw once in a field at Llanwenarth squatting on a stool before a canvas with his brushes, paints and easel, painting a hedge so far as I could see.

It was a surprise, then, when I came across T.S. Eliot's little poem 'Usk' after Wyn had put me onto him in sixth form. My head was full of 'Prufrock', 'Portrait of a Lady', 'Rhapsody on a Windy Night', 'The Waste Land', none of which I could understand but whose music was thrilling,

Huge sea-wood fed with copper
Burned green and orange, framed by the coloured stone
In which sad light a carvèd dolphin swam.

What did it mean? It didn't matter.

But 'Usk' was disappointing. It seemed frigid and superficial. It had nothing to do with the living, breathing river that I knew, whose bullheads I caught, whose dace quivered in shoals from end to end of flood pools where they were trapped. David Jones's Llanthony paintings, too, seemed insipid after I discovered them. They captured nothing of the brooding depth of the hills no matter how good they may be in other ways. But Eliot and Jones were outsiders, picnickers in my world where people got on with their lives unbothered by poetry or paintings.

So when I read Raymond Williams' autobiographical novel *Border Country*, bought I see in 1962 when I was in my second year at Birmingham University, it was a revelation. Here thinly disguised were Pandy and Abergavenny, with the Junction and Monmouth Road Stations, and my own school King Henry's where Raymond Williams had been a pupil twenty years before me, though he had been a 'Rustican' while I as a town boy had been an 'Oppidan'. But there was more. My father's brother Don, who kept the village store and post office on the Mardy, had been a porter at Pontrilas station in 1926 when Raymond Williams's father was a signalman just down the line at Pandy. In the tight-knit world of railwaymen in those days, they may well have known one another.

In 1987 I interviewed Raymond Williams for *Planet*. It was the first and only time I met him, in his cottage deep in the Black Mountains. We had lunch and I tape-recorded the interview about his novel

People of the Black Mountains. I was impressed by the depth of his historical knowledge of the Mountains and his sensitivity to the nuances of weather and mood in the hills. But what I took from the meeting was a sense of how his years in Cambridge, his numerous publications and international reputation had barely changed him. He retained the peculiar bur of the Mountains that is a blend of Herefordshire and South Wales and there was, as we would say in Abergavenny, no side to him at all. We talked of King Henry's and the masters we had in common despite the twenty-year gap in our education there, and instead of feeling daunted as I expected I felt at ease.

So Abergavenny and the Black Mountains *could* be written about after all — that was what I drew from reading *Border Country* all those years before I met the author. Yet I shelved that knowledge. It didn't occur to me that I might write about the town and the hills myself. Writing was what other people did.

The Bible

How much of the Bible have I read? Genesis several times, also the Gospels; Job and Revelations; Ecclesiastes — all in the Authorised version. I've consulted the Bible frequently using Cruden's *Concordance* but I have never read it from cover to cover. I did set out to do so once but foundered on Leviticus and Numbers. So not much, is the answer.

Yet I feel I know the Bible well because I heard its words every school-day of my life on the lips of the nuns at St Michael's and during morning assembly at King Henry's; every Sunday at St Mary's Church too during my enforced attendance, until I broke away after my confirmation at the age of fifteen. The years had a rhythm that progressed from 'Let there be light' to 'He is not here, but risen'. It was different from the rhythm of the seasons played out across the Black Mountains, yet the two were somehow coterminous, the one real and living, the other a series of tableaux, of prayerful attitudes.

At Christmas they intersected on a dark cold night when the grammar school held its carol service in the Baptist Chapel. Outside was the bronze sculpture of the First World War soldier leaning on his rifle and looking wearily down Frogmore Street. His back was turned to the Chapel, his bones rotting in a war grave or lost in the mud of the trenches.

But no one thought of that as parents turned in at the Chapel doors and we boys were paraded in our blazers and ties, with the choir, which included me at one time, up in the balcony ready to perform.

Here cold mid-winter came in contact with the bright star leading Three Wise Men to a dimly lit stable, Joseph and Mary, the warm breath of cows, and the baby who was Saviour of the World. In St Michael's I had always been fascinated by the Nativity crib with its painted wooden people and animals which the nuns set out on a table, at chin height as it seems in memory, for us children.

... and, lo, the star, which they saw in the east, went before them, till it came and stood over where the young child was.

When they saw the star, they rejoiced with exceeding great joy.

And when they were come into the house, they saw the young child with Mary his mother, and fell down, and worshipped him: and when they had opened their treasures, they presented unto him gifts; gold, and frankincense, and myrrh.

The words echoed in the vault of the Chapel and the carols rang out clear; darkness pressing at the windows but kept at bay for now.

When I think about the Bible, my mind teems with characters, stories and phrases — Abraham sacrificing Isaac, Jacob and the coat of many colours, Noah and the great flood, the Word brooding over the darkness, Belshazzar's feast and the writing on the wall, Daniel in the lions' den, the fall of Jericho, the great star Wormwood, the seven plagues of Egypt, Jesus whipping the moneylenders, cursing the fig tree, walking on water, Pilate washing his hands, 'My God, why hast thou forsaken me?' 'And on the third day He rose again'. It is a colourful, violent world, full of sorrow and malevolence, ruled over by Yahweh, the puppet master, a world Jesus tried to subvert with his message of love.

This world never had anything to do with me. My world was Abergavenny, the hills and the river, a real world you could feel and hear and see. The Bible world was one adults imposed upon you, told you was important, was part of their rituals you couldn't challenge or deny. Now I see it with other eyes as the jumbled myths, legends, ritual codes and world history of Iron Age communities of the Near East which brought forth three monotheistic religions that are among the plagues of mankind.

Nonetheless I am glad I had that background, that initiation however grudging on my part, into the wellsprings of Christianity. It gave me my first challenge in independent thinking, a primitive grounding in logic as I disputed free will versus predestination, the veracity or otherwise of miracles. It also gave me an essential background to European culture of the past fifteen hundred years. If you know nothing of the Bible, how do you read *Paradise Lost*, or Donne or Herbert, or Manley Hopkins, or that satirist of Christian hypocrisy, Caradoc Evans?

The well-meaning 'comparative religion' taught in schools today won't give you any of this. It has more to do with social engineering, creating tolerance in a multi-ethnic society by providing insight into different cultures and belief systems. It tells you nothing about the *imperative* of religion, how it controls people's lives and is used to control the lives of others. It traces the skin and conceals the beating heart.

The Outsider

Colin Wilson's *The Outsider* was published in 1956 and I must have read it a year or so later. I can't remember now how I came across it. I don't think Wyn recommended it, and *The Outsider* is not the sort of book that would have been reviewed in *The Daily Express* or *The News of the World*, the newspapers my parents took at the time. It caused a stir, not least because of the romantic story of how Colin Wilson wrote it in the Reading Room of the British Museum by day, while sleeping rough on Hampstead Heath at night. *The Outsider* was one of those books that was in the air and somehow it came to my attention in Abergavenny where I bought it in a cheap paperback — from Smith's presumably as there was no other bookshop in the town.

From my point of view I discovered it at just the right moment. At seventeen or eighteen I had rebelled against my mother's notional Christianity and had long since stopped attending St Mary's. I was searching for something but I didn't know what; something that would define me in opposition to the conservative world of my shopkeeper parents and what seemed the stifling strictures of school and town.

Perhaps I had seen it on the bookstall at Smith's and the title had attracted me. The book started me on a course of reading — Kafka's *The Trial* and *The Castle*, Camus's *The Outsider* and *The Plague*, Sartre's *Nausea*, T.E. Lawrence's *The Seven Pillars of Wisdom*, Van Gogh's letters to his brother, almost all of Herman Hesse.

I don't remember anything about the argument of *The Outsider* and I doubt if I understood much of it at the time; I have never had a head for abstraction and have never been able to read philosophy. I couldn't have defined existentialism even though it was fundamental to the book, and I cannot do so now. It was the idea embodied in the title that attracted me because it appeared to legitimise my feeling of alienation from the world around me. You could *be* an 'outsider' and there were people who had been it before me — it was all right, even if it wasn't all right in the eyes of Abergavenny.

I kept my copy for years but never re-read it and somewhere among many moves between Wales, England and Denmark I lost it or discarded it. I would almost certainly find it unreadable now — *The Outsider* was of its time, like the novels of Herman Hesse; but I am grateful to Colin Wilson for allowing me to see that the confusion of feelings and thoughts I struggled with had antecedents, and that these might help explain me to myself.

Foochow

My friends Tom and Roynon Collings lived in Foochow, Woodland Road, which was just up from our house on the Hereford Road. Tom and Roynon didn't go to King Henry's but were day pupils at Monmouth School, travelling to Monmouth by bus. So we had different routines and though they lived four hundred yards away I only got to know them when as teenagers we all attended Saint Mary's Church youth club.

My motive for going to the whitewashed outbuilding at the side of the church had nothing to do with God — Monica, who I was courting, went there, and it was a chance to be with her on a weekday evening. There was table tennis and at the end of the evening the curate Chris Seralis read a bit from the Bible and led us in a prayer. I could endure that. It was Monica I had my eyes on.

One evening she turned up in a tight-fitting red dress that followed every curve of her body. She must have been sixteen. It was the kind of dress Jayne Mansfield wore in *Too Hot to Handle*. I knew this because on the annual trip to Stratford which Wyn organised for English Literature sixth formers, some of us slipped out of a matinee performance at the theatre to go and see it. I can't remember which Shakespeare play we absented ourselves from, but I remember Jayne, sashaying down a suburban street in a dress like Monica's. She passed an ice man making a delivery. He looked up and his hands sizzled through the block of ice. She passed a milkman. His spectacles shattered and two pints of milk boiled over in his hands. 'Hey little girl — you with the red dress on!' Pine Top Smith knew all about it on 'Pine Top's Boogie Woogie' that I played on a 78 in our front room.

Roynon too, as I discovered, was plagued by sex and passion, courting L— D—. One evening while the two of us were mooning around and our girlfriends were doing something else, he persuaded me to walk up to Lansdowne Road where L— lived. We stopped before the house. It was dark and there was a light on in the downstairs front room; the curtains had not been drawn. Roynon decided to creep up and take a peek at the beloved. A moment later I heard his footsteps running hard down the path. He had poked his head up over the sill to be confronted by the eyes of a man entirely unknown to him eating his supper.

Foochow is not a common name for a house in Abergavenny. It had belonged to a couple who had been missionaries in China. You didn't change house names then as you do now, so there it was on the painted iron gate, 'Foochow'.

Mr Collings, Roynon and Tom's father, had been brought up in Pontnewynydd. He was a police inspector who worked at the police HQ on the corner of Hereford Road and Lower Monk Street. Some days I would see him cycling home for dinner on his big black bike as I was walking home to mine. His uniform was black and his peaked cap was black, and he wore sturdy hobnailed boots that he called 99ers. 'That's what you need, John, a pair of 99ers.' He was a large man with a bull neck and a loud voice. Even when he laughed and was trying to be pleasant there was an air of menace about him and I knew from Roynon he had a violent temper. So I was always wary of him.

Mrs Collings was a short plump woman from Pembrokeshire. Like many women of her generation she lived for her boys, and deep down I think resented the fact that as they grew into men they had lives beyond the home. When the three of us started going to pubs she would tell Tom and Roynon not to be late getting back as she would have fried brains on toast ready for them and didn't want them spoiled. When the boys married and moved away there was trouble with the wives. Tom married an American and Roynon someone from the English middle class. Neither wife I suspect understood Mrs Collings and her restricted world which expressed itself in not too subtle Mam-like manipulation, the only weapon she had.

Mr Collings was a big man at Saint Mary's, a member of the choir whose voice boomed loudly over everyone else's. In Canon Davies's time, Saint Mary's was Low Church but Mr Collings's mentality was Calvinistic Methodist, and it strikes me now as odd that he was a member of the Church in Wales. But there he was every Sunday in procession with the choir, his 99ers shining black under the cassock.

Apart from gardening and religion, I don't think he had any interests and when he retired from the force he must have been at a loose end. He took to walking in the hills and sometimes I'd meet him at the foot of the Sugar Loaf pounding along, swishing his stick at the bracken, timing himself and trying to beat his record of the day before.

One morning when he was sixty-two or -three he knelt down to see to the living room fire and keeled over with a heart attack. I stood in our front room the day of the funeral and saw the hearse and the black car with Tom, Roynon and their mother pass down Hereford Road to the church.

When it came to university I sat the scholarship exam at Wyn's old college UCW Aberystwyth but was unsuccessful. In any case my grades at A-level were disappointing — B in English, C in History, D in Geography. The C and D didn't surprise me. My only interest was English and I did the other two on sufferance because you had to have three A-levels. I persuaded my parents to let me stay on a third year to improve my grades and for some reason was allowed to drop Geography, which suited me fine. For a whole year I had the luxury of tutorials with Wyn, with History on the side. In the exams I improved my grades to an A and a B. This, combined with two days of intensive exams and interviews at Birmingham University, secured me a place to study English there.

Tom and Roynon went from Monmouth School to Oxford, Tom to study Mathematics, and Roynon History, though he later changed to English. Mr Collings was immensely proud of this. 'It's the Mecca of Learning, John, the Mecca of Learning.'

The front room at Foochow was like most front rooms then, with a china cabinet on top of which were framed photos of the boys, upholstered easy chairs, a wall mirror, and a floral carpet, kept for 'best' except when we boys took it over as the only room we could be private in. Tom and Roynon were jazz enthusiasts, and although Roynon had a liking for what he considered the genuine, raw New Orleans jazz of George Lewis, both were deeply committed to modern jazz. It was through them that I first heard Charlie Parker, Miles Davies, Thelonious Monk, Chet Baker, Lenny Tristano, Dizzie Gillespie, Jimmy Giufre, Sonny Rollins, Harry Eddison, and many others.

At this time I was discovering the blues, and had 78s of Sleepy John Estes, Muddy Waters, Pine Top

Smith, Jesse James and 10-inch LPs of Blind Lemon Jefferson, Lead Belly, Jazz Gillum and whoever else I could find in catalogues at Young's Television and Record Shop on the corner of Market Street. Then I discovered a shop in London that sold made-to-order 12-inch acetate discs of blues. You chose a singer — Peetie Wheatstraw, say — and the shop sent you a typed list of titles from which you selected twelve to be made up into your own customised LP. The quality was poor, but through these stabs in the dark I heard Robert Johnson's 'Preaching Blues' in the late 1950s, several years before Columbia brought out the first commercial LP of his music.

Singers like Lemon Jefferson, Robert Johnson and Jesse James were deeply attractive because they articulated an emotional intensity which was a correlative to the churning feelings I had within me, especially regarding women and sex. This was very different from the ersatz emotions of 1950s pop or the older ballroom orchestra music my parents sometimes listened to on the radio. Genuineness became a touchstone in literature and music, whether it was Holden Caulfied exposing phonyness in New York or the lone bluesman articulating the intensity of black experience in the South.

Unlike jazz, however, which had magazines like *Jazz Journal* and books like Rudi Blesh's *Shining Trumpets* (Tom and Roynon subscribed to the one and had a copy of the other from a jazz book club) the blues was an unknown quantity. There were no books on the subject in Britain until Paul Oliver's *Blues Fell This Morning* and Samuel Charters' *The Country Blues* which were published in 1960. Nor was there any discography, so you had no idea how many recordings Blind Lemon or Sleepy John might have made. Each

78 or 10-inch LP shone an exciting light into an unknown world.

Somehow I found out that you could borrow records from the American Embassy library in London. In this way I came upon the field recordings of John and Alan Lomax made in the 1930s and '40s. This was another world again, of work songs recorded on prison farms like Parchman, Mississippi, of arhoolies or field hollers, of the rough and ready first recordings of Mackinley Morganfield who became Muddy Waters. You ordered from a catalogue and records came through the post in a hard box. You could keep them for, I think, a fortnight and then had to return them. These were Library of Congress recordings, some of them pressed on translucent raspberry-red vinyl, which added to their exotic status.

I don't think any of us realised what a significant time this was. The 1950s and early '60s were the last great innovative period in jazz when at Foochow we listened to the latest LPs by Thelonious Monk, Miles Davies, Charles Mingus, Harry Eddison, bought by Tom or Roynon after reading reviews in *Jazz Journal* or *Jazz Monthly*.

As for the blues, the 1950s were an age of discovery when youths like me woke up to a music that had been largely invisible to whites in the first half of the twentieth century. It was a music whose history had yet to be written. Most of us listening to the blues in the late 1950s probably did so in isolation, as I did in Abergavenny. It was some years before I met anyone else interested in the music. How many of us were there in 1958 in the USA and across Britain and Europe? A few hundred at most I would guess. But among them were Bob Dylan, Keith Richards, Eric Clapton and other singers and instrumentalists from the early years of rock, who forged a new music out of this hidden, poorly understood storehouse of black recordings.

After Mr Collings died, Mrs Collings lived on at Foochow. It must have been a lonely existence. She and Mr Collings had never socialised and I doubt they had any friends. There were only the visits of her boys to look forward to and these were frequently spoiled from her point of view by their exotic wives who vied for Tom and Roynon's affection and challenged her attempts at manipulative control.

Sometimes she would come to our house and we would see her face appear round the back garden door, smiling weakly. Loneliness must have driven her down the Hereford Road, for there had never been any contact while Mr Collings was alive. After some years she started to behave oddly. Back on holiday from Denmark where I worked in the 1970s I would go up to Foochow to see her or I might meet her on the Hereford Road. She had a Cheshire Cat smile of recognition, but her mind would drift off or she would repeat herself; she often seemed to be looking to a far horizon no one else could see.

Eventually she was diagnosed with Altzheimer's and ended up in Triley Court which had been converted into a nursing home. I visited her a few times, walking up the drive as I had many years before when I delivered the telegram. We met in the day-room which must have been a large reception room when the Court was a functioning country house. The home specialised in people with deteriorating brain functions like Mrs Collings. 'Oh, there are the monks,' she told me once, 'coming down the stairs. They're very good; they light my fire every morning.' She was sometimes more lucid, asking Roynon when she would be going home, never knowing that Foochow had already been sold. On one visit an old woman banged on the window panes, 'I want to go home; I want to go home'. A nurse tried to calm her. On another, a patient, perhaps the same one, 'escaped' and was making off down the drive, only to be overtaken and led back gently but firmly to her stately incarceration. You had to be careful where you sat. On one visit Tom sat on a chair whose seat was wet with urine. He cycled back to town with a wet backside. After hearing that, I examined the chairs carefully. Even so I once came away from the Court with my trousers stinking of stale urine from sitting in a chair that had seemed dry and innocent enough. All the residents at Triley Court must have yearned in lucid moments to return home but for them on their slow journey into confusion and oblivion there was no home but this.

When at last she died Mrs Collings was buried from St Teilo's Church on the Mardy. She had quarrelled with the vicar of St Mary's some years before, a quarrel she perpetuated to the edge of the grave. Tom, by then a clergyman himself, conducted the service. My brother drove him and Roynon behind the hearse up the Hereford Road to the Mardy in his light brown Reliant Robin.

History

At King Henry's Wyn Binding taught History to O-level. We studied the WJEC syllabus on 'History of the British Empire' with a subsidiary on 'Welsh History'. I enjoyed the British Empire component. I was a stamp collector by then, specialising in British Empire and Commonwealth, and spent a lot of my time poring over the Stanley Gibbons' 'Commonwealth' catalogue, with its hard covers bound in deep red linen. I could relate the stamps to the history of the Raj and the colonisation of West and East Africa. Empire history was full of battles and intrigues and characters like Warren Hastings and Robert Clive, as well as men of action on the sidelines such as Denys Reitz, whose memoir of the Boer Wars, *Commando*, with its deep blue Penguin covers had been recommended by Wyn. The syllabus ended with those wars, however, so we never learned about resistance to Empire and the process of decolonisation that was going on around us. I could read about that, however, in my parents' *Daily Express* with its 'exposure' of the iniquitous Mau Mau in Kenya and their attacks on 'innocent' white settlers. Jomo Kenyatta, Gamal Abdel Nasser, Kwame Nkrumah formed a string of hate figures for the petit-bourgeois tabloids at the time.

I was less enthusiastic about Welsh History which I remember as the history of Nonconformism from the eighteenth century to the Revival of 1904, consisting more or less of lists of preachers and their doings. Perhaps it was the way Wyn taught it; perhaps his heart wasn't in it — mine certainly wasn't since, by this time, I was in rebellion against Christianity and its intrusion into my life.

Wyn, however, could only teach History as far as O-level because his degree was in English. This must have given the Headmaster a problem since there was no master with a History degree who could take the subject at A-level. The solution was to send the two or three of us who continued with History up to the High School for Girls in Harold Road where we were taught by Miss Hughes, a History graduate from UCW Aberystwyth. There was a reciprocal arrangement whereby girls studying A-level Biology came down to us to be taught by Mrs Jones since the High School had no teacher with a degree in Biology. Among them was Monica who I would glimpse sometimes as she entered the school gates. If our eyes met she would give me a smile that might be called enigmatic like that of the *Mona Lisa*, a painting I have never liked perhaps for this reason

Going to the High School was an ordeal. There was the interesting freedom of walking out of the gates during school hours and strolling up Pen-y-Pound and Avenue Road, but entering a building full of girls required a degree of nerve. A dozen giggling faces would appear round each classroom door, only to be snatched back with a lot of pushing and shoving as we passed. We'd been told to hang our coats and caps on hooks in the corridor, which we did. But this was too much of a temptation for the third form girls in the adjoining classroom who would sneak out and snaffle one or more of the caps. Our frustration as we looked up and down the corridor knowing what had happened but not what to do about it was evidently a great joke. We were caught in a bind. It was impossible to walk back to the grammar school without our caps but it was equally impossible to walk into a classroom of thirty girls and demand their return. Eventually a hand would appear and fling the cap or caps toward us quick-as-a-flash, after which we left to the sound of more giggling, pushing and shoving in the classroom doorways behind us.

Almost all subjects up to O-level involved the dictation of notes by the teachers, including Wyn, but in sixth form there was a much freer spirit of enquiry and note taking and dictation more or less ceased. This development hadn't reached Miss Hughes at the High School, however, where History classes mostly consisted of the endless taking down of notes on the Thirty Years War, the War of Austrian Succession, or Cromwell and the English Civil War. When this became too much, the girls in the class had a way of diverting her into telling anecdotes about her undergraduate years in Aberystwyth. Miss Hughes was a spinster, perhaps fifty years old, with grey hair, ruddy cheeks, and a gentle disposition. 'Tell us about the visit from the Japanese ambassador, Miss,' one of them would say, and Miss Hughes would forget Frederick the Great, to lose herself in her youth. She particularly remembered the ambassador's wife who had been dressed in a wonderful kimono, and she would describe again the quality of the cloth, its intricate embroidery, the way in which the lady held a delicate fan, the bowing and formality of the occasion. This must have been some time in the 1930s. It had been a wonderful day... but then it was back to dictation and there was no sound except the rustle of pens and Miss Hughes's voice as she read out a sentence, paused while we wrote it down, read out another, paused again. History didn't appeal to me but it was necessary to my plan which was to go to university, study English, and do nothing but read novels and poems for three years.

The girls in the History class overawed us. I don't think they meant to, but they were young women while we were in many ways boys. I was going out with Monica by this time but hardly understood the nature of women. All we knew was the sexual drive that impelled us toward them.

Because of this we even endured the annual school dances held for fifth and sixth formers at Christmas, one at the grammar school and one at the high school. Dancing still meant ballroom dancing, and each year, starting in November, there would be a weekly dancing class in the grammar school gym when girls came down from the high school to partner us in the waltz, the fox trot and the quick step. The aim was to break us boys in, but I don't think we got beyond the waltz which was comparatively easy — *one*-two-three *one*-two-three *one*-two-three. For the rest we held a girl stiffly in our arms, feet shuffling to the rhythm, hoping not to tread on her toes.

Although ballroom dancing looks staid, it is more sexually charged than rock dancing where you dance in front of your partner without touching her. To place your hand on a girl's back, with your right hand holding her left hand, to be so close to her face and hair, to smell her perfume, was strange and alluring and embarrassing all in one. As a result, we danced like marionettes, trying not to look in the girl's eyes.

On the night of the dance itself, which at the grammar school took place in the joint-classrooms where we held assembly, its floor specially polished for the occasion, all us boys felt extra-clumsy in our suits and ties, while the girls were transformed, unrecognisable in dresses and ball gowns with floral designs, or in shining pinks, greens or blues.

At one dance Monica wore a kingfisher blue off-the-shoulder dress, with blue stockings and blue high heels. I couldn't stop looking at her. Another time, while I waited for her, watching the crowded floor, someone came and told me P— J— had been kissing her in the cloakroom. Almost immediately, he came back into the dance hall, walked up to me and insisted on shaking my hand. It was a double insult and I should have slapped him, but with a hundred people present and teachers standing around watchfully, I lamely submitted. You never forget insults. Were I to meet him today I would be tempted to give him that slap retrospectively.

Occasionally girls who had left the previous summer came to the high school dance to see their old teachers and to show themselves off. Returning to Abergavenny after a first term at university they seemed mature beyond our reach. We could only look on. One such beautiful returnee wore a flared brown skirt. It must have been 1959 because we had persuaded the teachers to play rock 'n' roll in between 78s of Victor Sylvester and other ballroom orchestras. Perhaps it was 'Rock Around the Clock' or 'See You Later, Alligator' by Bill Haley and His Comets. The girl was out there in the middle of the dance floor, and every time her partner twirled her, her skirt rose in a wheel to her waist. She must have known, and known the effect it was having, as sixty pairs of male eyes followed her, like Moses gazing into the Promised Land.

In History at the high school I don't think we spoke to the girls once. We kept our heads down, retrieved our caps from the third formers and walked out of the gates into Harold Road. We knew what History was about; it was about sex.

Bus Conductor

Toward the end of my last term at King Henry's I heard that the Western Welsh were looking for a temporary bus conductor over the summer months. My friend John Lloyd heard of it too and we agreed to toss a coin to decide which of us should apply. I won, filled in a form, and got the job. That was in 1960.

Immediately, as is my habit, I panicked, believing that I wouldn't be able to do it. My arithmetic was appalling. How was I going to work out the complications of pounds, shillings and pence when giving change? My shopkeeper parents showed me. You don't try to subtract 2s 5d from £1 in your head. What you do is add up as you go along — 5d plus 7d equals 1 shilling. You place 7 pence in the passenger's hand. Then you go 1 shilling plus 4 equals 5, plus 5 equals 10 shillings, plus another 10 equals £1, handing these coins to the passenger. And there you have it — fare, 2s 5d; change, 17s and 7d. I wasn't quite convinced, but it worked, and within a few days I was handing out change as if I'd done it all my life.

Most of the bus routes from Abergavenny were operated by the Red & White Company, but the Western Welsh ran the buses from Brecon to Abergavenny and on to Pontypool as an outpost of their West Wales heartland. They had three shifts — from 7.30 in the morning to 3.30 in the afternoon, from 3.30 to 11.30 at night, and from 1.30 to 9.30 in the morning.

When I turned up at 7.30 on the first day, I was given a light grey Western Welsh summer jacket, a round green plastic conductor's licence with my number on it which had to be worn at all times, a leather money satchel, a set of timetables, a list of fares, and a metal ticket machine that weighed about 3 lbs. I felt panic rising in me again. How was I going to master all this? The ticket machine had three concentric dials for pounds, shillings and pence. If the fare was 3/6d, you set the pound dial to 0, the shilling dial to 3 and the pence dial to 6. You also had to remember to set 'single' or 'return', then you turned the handle on the right-hand side of the machine and the ticket emerged from a slot which you tore off and gave to the passenger together with the change.

On top of this, you had to learn the routes of which there were effectively three — down to Pontypool and back, then on without stopping up to Brecon either by the main road through Crickhowell and Bwlch, or via the back road, turning off at Crickhowell over the Usk and along the canal through Llangynidr, Talybont and Llanfrynach. The Brecon bus travelled the main and back roads alternately every hour.

That first morning I was put in the care of a conductor and at 7.30 we set off for Pontypool with me following him up and down the bus watching what he did. Then it was up to Brecon and back and he handed over to me. At first I was slow and clumsy, there seemed so much to learn — even things like how to keep your balance in a bus as it swayed and bumped along country roads. There was a trick to that, however, which the conductor showed me — you lean back pressing the crack of your buttocks firmly into the seat behind you, standing stiff-legged with feet apart. This gives you sufficient purchase to allow you to keep your hands free while giving out tickets and taking money.

After a couple of days I was considered trained. From then on I turned up at the bus station to join the big maroon single-decker with my driver who wound the destination board to 'PONTYPOOL'. We took on passengers and then drove up the Monmouth Road to the Pontypool turn while I went along the bus taking fares. After I had done that I would go and chat to the driver, stepping aside as passengers got on or off at stops along the way.

Some of the drivers were taciturn and you left them alone, but most wanted to talk, Charley O'Brien in particular. He was a thin, neat man with dark hair and a trim moustache. Charley's wife had died young and he had brought up their son and daughter alone. He was immensely proud of them and kept me updated on their achievements, but he was also a man of theories and fixed ideas. Charley was convinced there were people living on the moon, and we might spend the whole of the journey to Brecon discussing this. I pointed out that there was no atmosphere on the moon, but Charley thought this didn't matter as they might be living underground which of course explained why we couldn't see any signs of life — thus effectively answering another counter-argument of mine. This was before the moon landings. I don't know whether they dented Charley's theory, though I can imagine him saying, 'Well they were only on the surface for a few minutes, weren't they.'

Charley was something of a prankster too. 'Watch this,' he said one afternoon as we approached the hump-backed bridge over the Usk at Llanellen. A couple of holidaymakers on the back seat had just poured themselves cups of tea out of a flask. Charley increased speed as we reached the bridge. Up came the front of the bus over the hump — down it went like a rollercoaster — then up went the back end in a flip which lifted the holiday couple out of their seats and the tea out of their plastic cups. In the mirror I watched as the tea stood weightless in mid air until gravity intervened and it fell back with a splash in their laps. I could see a lot of mopping up being done. Charley glanced at me with his Clark Gable 'tash and smiled and we drove on toward Pontypool as if nothing had happened.

Trevor Bowen, a quiet man who lived in a council house on Park Avenue just across the way from us, would tell me of the 1930s when, if the bus was crowded, passengers drew back the sun roof which buses had then and sat around the edges with legs dangling down into the bus.

Jack Case, white haired and softly spoken, told me the secrets of growing prize chrysanthemums as the bus nosed up the long climb to Bwlch, easing over the pass into the country beyond. Every driver had his particular interest. One, whose name I forget, was a keen vegetable gardener and added to his wages by selling his produce to known passengers along the way. A luggage rack ran the length of the bus, and on some trips the front end would be packed with punnets of tomatoes, bags of potatoes, lettuces, ready for his customers. Once we came back on the last bus from Brecon with a used front door stowed on the back seat.

The shift from 1.30am to 9.30am was in some ways best because it was the most varied and exciting. You did the morning and afternoon shifts for six days each but the night shift for only three. The Western Welsh had a contract with the Royal Mail to carry the post from Abergavenny to Brecon and at 1.30am we would drive up to Abergavenny Monmouth Road Station, park the bus, and wait for the down train which would arrive at 2.00 with mail from the North.

As the bags were hurled out of the guard's van we caught them and loaded them onto a four-wheeled porter's trolley which we then trundled round to the bus. The emergency door at the back was opened and the driver handed the bags up to me and I stacked them on the back seats. We then had an hour and a half to wait for the up train from Cardiff, settling down to doze as best we could sprawled across two seats, the bus half-lit by the lamps outside the station.

When we heard the train's piston-beat and its chuff-chuff-chuff down the line, we roused ourselves and went back out to the platform, and the process of unloading and loading started all over again until the back of the bus was piled high with mail bags.

By then it was 4.00am. The driver climbed into his cab, I sat on the front passenger seat and we drove off through the empty streets of Abergavenny and out of town, the mellow light of the headlamps sweeping over hedgerows and the grey road. There was no traffic as we trundled through Glangrwyney, past the barracks at Cwrt-y-gollen and through a sleeping Crickhowell, the mountains sombre bulwarks against the summer sky that became paler as we approached Bwlch until it was dawn and we entered what seemed a washed-out world that was no doubt a projection of our own tiredness.

At Brecon Post Office we unloaded the bus and went into a small rest room, sat down at its bare table and unpacked our sandwiches and flasks of tea or coffee. A postman would come in now and then and chat to the driver. One I remember had a gripe against the world and only one adjective to express it. It was the first time I had heard swearing of that kind and deep down I was shocked by the man's coarseness, though later in life I was to become hardened and often coarse myself.

At 6.30 it was time to go. The driver backed out of the Post Office yard and we drove round to the Abergavenny bus stop on the main square ready for the first passengers of the day. From Abergavenny we manned the second bus down to Pontypool and back after which our shift was finished. This left the rest of the day free and if the weather was good I might go home, change into tennis whites and play five sets with Tom or Roynon Collings on the courts in Bailey Park. In the evening I might go out with Monica. I could do this for the first two days, sleeping maybe three and a half hours a night, but after I came off the second night I had a pervading sense of fuzziness in my body.

This led to disaster on one occasion when on the third night of the shift I woke to the alarm clock at 1.00am and thought I would just have five minutes more. The next thing there was a bang-bang-bang on the front door. I knew immediately what had happened and rushed downstairs to find Trevor Bowen on the doorstep and the big maroon bus parked on Hereford Road. He had met the down train, loaded the bus by himself and then come to get me. There was no time to wash or brush my teeth, I just dressed, grabbed my sandwiches, and Trevor and I drove back to the station to wait for the up train. I never did that again.

Mostly nothing happened on the long drive through the night and summer dawn to Brecon, but one night as we approached Glangrwyney we saw a car turned over on its roof at the side of the road. The driver stopped the bus and I expected him to get out and look, but he sat firmly in his cab and told me to. The road is overhung with trees at this point, so it was doubly dark as I got down from the bus. The car was old, with a bulk that suggested it was very heavy.

I had to get down on my hands and knees to peer through the shattered driver's window, hoping I wouldn't come face to face with the dead, but there was no one in the upside-down world of the interior, so I got back in the bus and we drove on. I never found out what had happened.

Another time, on the last bus from Brecon, as Jack Case and I drove past the Lamb and Flag and down the slope to Abergavenny, we were stopped by a line of cars. Jack and I got out. Just ahead we could hear two women screaming hysterically. There had been an accident and a car was canted over on its side in the hedge bank with people standing around while the women screamed and sobbed. Mr Case suggested I go behind the bus and warn following cars to stop. I did this until the queue had backed up to the entrance to Lower Pentre Lane. When I walked back to the bus I found it had gone, waved on by the police I discovered later when I met Mr Case on his way home through Abergavenny's deserted streets. It was too late to pay in, as you did at the end of every shift, taking the coins and notes from your satchel and entering the amount in pounds, shillings and pence on a paying-in slip. You double-checked this against the amount indicated on the ticket machine and if the two sums tallied, you paid in to the Red & White cashier at the bus station. If you were short, you had to make up the sum out of your own pocket. If you were over, you were expected to hand in the surplus to the company. No conductor ever did this, as I quickly discovered. Usually my figures tallied, though sometimes I was a few pence short, and once a magnificent ten shillings over.

One journey which none of the drivers or conductors liked was the last bus from Pontypool to Abergavenny on Friday and Saturday evenings. We would turn up at the stand in Pontypool at about 10.45pm and by the time we left at 11.00 the bus was full. There were some ordinary passengers but the majority were big, beefy rough-and-tumble young men, some with girls, who had been drinking for the last four hours and were now on their way to Little Mill where there was a dance hall with a late licence. The men would settle down in their seats, arms folded, legs apart, most of them with 'duck's arse' hair-do's and sideburns that extended to a level with the base of their ear-lobes. As we pulled out of the bus station I went along the bus trying to collect fares, but some of the regular drivers and conductors had warned me — don't push it, and if they won't pay, leave them alone. One ploy they used was to 'fall asleep' as I approached, so when I stood over them and said 'Fares, please', I was met with the smiling face of a slumbering man with biceps like Popeye. In the beginning I would insist for form's sake and repeat 'Fares, please' and might gently tap a shoulder. Nothing would happen, of course, and I moved on. I resented this but I knew there had been trouble in the past, and I wasn't going to get beaten up for the sake of a 1/6d fare. Some paid, but most never did and got off at Little Mill with an arrogant swagger. Then we moved off and everyone left on the bus breathed more freely.

The Company must have got wind of this because one Saturday an Inspector joined us as we left Abergavenny. We were going to sort this problem out, he told me. He was a small, sharp little man, who met the bus from time to time in unexpected places to inspect the tickets. He rarely smiled and I don't think the regular drivers and conductors liked him much — his job, after all, was to catch them out. As we drove to Pontypool he outlined his plan. I was to collect the money for the fares while he came behind me and gave out the tickets. This didn't sound like a good plan at all, and I suggested that *he* took the fares while I gave out the tickets. With a certain reluctance he agreed. At Pontypool the bus filled up and at 11.00pm we backed away from the stand. The Inspector set off up the aisle with my money satchel while I came behind with the ticket machine. The Pontypool boys followed the same ploy as always. Nobody could have been more deeply or soundly asleep and not even a gentle shaking by an Inspector could wake them. He had been very determined on the way down but faced with a six-foot, fifteen-stone glass- or steel-worker, even he wasn't stupid enough to force the issue. So the Pontypool boys 'slept' as usual until the bus pulled up at the Little Mill stop. The Inspector never came on the last bus again and we heard no more about it.

My favourite route was on the back road to Brecon, driving along the leafy narrow lane through Talybont and Llanfrynach, crossing hump-backed bridges over the canal with glimpses of its unruffled brown water. The drivers on this route knew their passengers. Sometimes we would stop when there was no one there. Why are we stopping? I would ask. Mrs Roberts will be here in a minute was the answer, and soon there she would be hurrying down a lane from a farmhouse two fields off. I liked this sense of ease, of feeling that life has no hurry. I have rarely encountered it since. When I left Abergavenny at the end of that summer to go to university I embarked on a period of twenty years' living in cities where nobody waited for anyone. From then on, it could be said, I lived on my nerves.

I loved working on the buses, the way the atmosphere changed depending on the composition of the passengers and the driver you were with; how going down to Pontypool you came to the edge of the industrial south, while travelling up to Brecon you went deeper and deeper into the Mid Wales hill country. It was my world then, I was a part of it.

As well as the familiar passengers there were also the strangers like the young Frenchman who got on at Abergavenny wanting to go to Breesón. Breesón? I checked my timetable; I had never heard of that stop. I asked the driver. He didn't know. Then suddenly I understood — ah, Brecon. Yes, he agreed, Breesón. I gave him his ticket. There was, too, the attractive girl, a sixth former at the Convent School for Girls in Abergavenny, reading a book on her way to Pontypool. It was rare to find anyone with a book on the buses so I was curious and tried to see what it was. The bus was almost empty but a motherly woman two seats back was amused, mistaking my interest. 'He's looking at you,' she said with a smile. I was embarrassed and must have blushed, but I had seen she was reading Conrad — *Victory*, I think — and I warmed to her, not for her looks as the middle-aged woman thought.

At the end of my first year at Birmingham University I applied to the Western Welsh again and got hired for a second summer. But the age of the bus conductor was coming to an end and when I applied in the summer of 1962 I was told the Western Welsh had gone over to one-man buses — driver and conductor rolled into one; manpower costs reduced by half.

Tennis

Tennis was the only sport I was good at, though I enjoyed cross-country running. For one whole winter, Tom, Roynon, their neighbour Don Gunter and myself ran three or four nights a week on a circuit — up the Ross Road past the old Junction Station and Maindiff Court, then left across the lane that led to the Mardy and back down the Hereford Road, a distance of about three and a half miles, half of it up a steep incline. It wasn't meant to be a race but of course it became one, with Tom or Roynon usually winning, me third, and Don at the rear, his feet going *slap-slap-slap* in the dark behind me.

It was tennis I liked best, though, and in summer, if the weather was fine, I played almost every day, either on the tarmac court at school or on the clay or grass courts at the top end of Bailey Park. These were kept in good condition and the grass courts were fast. There was a wooden pavilion where you could change. Since I lived a short way from the park, however, I usually changed at home. In the 1950s tennis was popular. There was a club in Pen-y-pound and another in the park. I never joined either, but played with Tom or Roynon, booking a court the day before at the park keeper's hut. Everyone wore whites and I enjoyed the ritual of changing into tennis shirt and shorts, white socks and tennis shoes.

I enjoyed, too, the ritual of the match — the warm-up, then easing your way into the first game, gauging where the sun was and how far it would get in your eyes. There was the satisfying *pock* when you hit a good forehand and placed the ball exactly where you intended, or hit a first-service ace. Tom, Roynon and I were evenly matched and every game was played to win. But I also liked pitting myself against my own body, against the sweat and aching muscles as we entered a fifth set — and the surroundings on a sunny day with the Little Skirrid, the Blorenge, the Deri, the Rholben, in a semi-circle, turning the park into a green arena.

The best tennis ever was when I got invited to play doubles with Wyn Binding, Gwyn Jones PE, and Dr Griffiths whose Georgian house and surgery were on Pen-y-pound, opposite the grammar school. Dr Griffiths had his own grass court, the finest court I ever played on. Wyn, Mr Jones and Dr Griffiths were all extremely good players — Wyn had been university champion at Aberystwyth — and the quality of their game upped mine. There was no room for a loose shot and you paid at the net for a moment's hesitation. After the game, Dr Griffiths took us through the French windows into his large, cool sitting room where we sank into big armchairs and drank fresh lemonade — something I had never tasted before — while the men talked and I listened, on the edge of a world very different from my own.

In my last year in sixth form, I had my one sporting triumph — winning the annual KHGS tennis tournament. I had reached the semi-finals before, but in 1960 I got to the final against Jeremy Price who I knew was the better player, particularly at the net. Wyn, however, coached me and gave me good advice — keep Jeremy away from the net, don't try passing shots because he will intercept them; lob and force him to the baseline where you can match him shot for shot. I did as Wyn said and against the odds I won, my name engraved on a shield on the base of the trophy which I kept for a year.

When you think about good times in the past it is almost inevitable that you romanticise them, memory being a treacherous filter. Even so, I am sure the 1950s were a good time to be young in Abergavenny. Bailey Park is a symbol of what I mean. The park keeper in his hut was arbiter of what went on — dogs had to be on a leash, bicycles had to be pushed not ridden, rowdy behaviour was not tolerated. If the tennis courts were crowded you were called in when your hour was up, otherwise you could play on, paying extra at the end. Everyone knew the rules and those rules gave order to the park; within them you were free. Eventually, however, the keeper's post was axed and Bailey Park followed him in a slow decline. When I visited a few years ago the high wire mesh surrounding the tennis courts lay crumpled on the ground, the courts vandalised and abandoned. The pavilion had been vandalised too and partially burned down, its charred remains blocked off by a security fence. Part of the box hedge around the bowling green had been burned and the outdoor swimming pool where I had swum every summer was locked, its flaking walls topped with barbed wire.

Thinking

The grammar school taught me how to think independently, to examine a proposition and draw my own conclusions. In sixth form Wyn Binding expected us to have ideas about the books we were reading and to be able to express them. He taught us how to write clearly and how to marshal evidence. There was no excuse for sloppy writing or wilful obscurity.

Wyn also analysed newspaper articles and advertisements from time to time to show how what you read cannot always be trusted, how you have to distinguish between what something purports to say and what it is really saying. In other words, he introduced us to propaganda. At this time I was also reading Orwell's *Animal Farm*, *1984*, and *Homage to Catalonia*. I began to understand how the world is manipulated around you all the time; how politicians especially are master propagandists; how you have to be on guard against the coercive power of words in the hands of those who seek to control you.

I would like to think this was one of the grammar schools' most important legacies in the post-war years, but if it was it had only a limited effect. Today language is misused more than ever, mostly by those who have always misused it, but across such a range of media that the abuse of language, and thinking, is a more or less permanent intrusion in our lives. There seems no way to subvert this other than through education, but when the universities have been overtaken by an administrative system that spouts business-speak, when academics in the humanities and social sciences write in the most arcane, obfuscating way, and when successive governments erode the authority and independence of teachers through a state of perpetual revolution, I doubt the education system is up to it. There are good teachers still in every school and university, but they are marginalised. Shortly after I left the grammar school, Wyn Binding moved to Barry Training College and from there to Trinity College, Carmarthen, where he was a colleague of Raymond Garlic. Toward the end of their careers at Trinity Wyn and Raymond felt alienated from the business ethos of the college administration which neither understood nor cared for the educational ideals by which they had lived and taught. I know lecturers and former lecturers at Coleg Harlech and at the universities in Wales who feel the same.

What I cannot do is think abstractly which is why I have never been able to read philosophy. I used to try — *The Myth of Sisyphus*, *Thus Spake Zarathustra*, Plato's *Dialogues* — but I never finished any of them. My mind is entirely visual. When I read a novel, words on the page are transformed immediately into images in my head — I 'see' what is being described in the finest detail. There are the abstract, dictionary words, and there is the visualisation springing from those words that I watch like a film. The process makes me a slow reader. For a long time I assumed everyone read like this, but talking to people who read much faster than me, I discovered they don't go through this visualising process, or at least not to the same degree. I have to believe them, though I am so locked into visualisation that I cannot imagine what reading of this kind might be like.

This may explain my resistance to science in King Henry's. What I remember of Chemistry is the deep black-blue of potassium permanganate crystals, the perfect silver spheres of mercury that we rolled across the laboratory tables. In Physics I remember passing a magnet under iron filings spread out on a piece of paper, fascinated by the way they sprang into beautiful patterns aligned to the magnetic field. I could never remember chemical formulae or equations.

Evolution

Monica and I were sitting on the sofa in the front room one day when she said, apropos of nothing, 'We live to eat to reproduce'. I had never expected such a proposition from her; I was shocked. But she was studying A-level Biology and I was not.

Would evolutionary theory have been part of the A-level syllabus in the late 1950s? I can only remember sixth formers dissecting rats and earthworms in the Biology lab amid the sharp stink of formaldehyde. She went on to study Biology at Retford Training College in Nottinghamshire and perhaps I have misremembered the date — perhaps she said this after we had left school.

In the late 1950s and throughout the '60s, along with many others in the humanities, I was anti-science. I was also totally ignorant of it. Only years later when I started reading up on evolutionary theory, palaeontology and palaeoanthropology did I understand what she meant. To me as a nineteen or twenty year old her remark had the same bleak, nihilistic ring as T.S. Eliot's Sweeney:

That's all, that's all, that's all, that's all,
Birth, and copulation, and death.

I was engrossed in the novels of D.H. Lawrence and my world was a Lawrentian one that refused the arid, sterile world of reason, as I saw it. I know I flared up at what she said because if it was true, if that is all there is, there could be no point to life. Literature, the Romantic landscape of the Black Mountains, passionate love — these were what mattered and gave the lie to the barren reductive view she had uttered. I can't remember if we actually argued about it. Perhaps she just gave me a Mona Lisa smile. Monica was merely expressing a fundamental biological truth; what Niles Eldredge has termed the economic and reproductive functions that govern all living organisms.

She was also a bell ringer and choir member at St Mary's, though I never discovered whether she was really a Christian. Every Sunday evening at 6.30 the bells would peel out — *Dee-dee-dee-dee-da-da-da-dum, Dee-dee-dee-dee-da-da-da-dum* — the sound drifting up Hereford Road to our front room where I waited for her. Then silence. Then a long hour — longer than being in church when I was a child — until she walked in through the back door.

Mrs Bennett was a clever dress-maker and made almost all Monica's clothes, including fashionable sheath dresses in shimmering nylon that came just above the knee. She would buy dress patterns and I watched sometimes as the two women knelt on the carpet, pinning the flimsy pattern to the rolled out piece of fabric.

Sitting there waiting, I knew Monica would be wearing her Sunday best and that it would be one of these dresses and that before she caught the last bus to Gilwern where she now lived, we would fumble with each other on the sofa, pleasure in each other's bodies giving way to deep frustration, on my part at least, because this was the 1950s.

Had I had the perspective, I might have asked myself whether beneath it all lay the reproductive urge that Monica had spoken of. I might dress it up in the black flames of Lawrentian desire, but what else had overwhelmed me at the age of fourteen or fifteen? And when my mother placed before me breakfast and dinner and tea, what was that? What lay beneath the pleasure of the meals themselves?

I could not answer any of these questions because I could not ask them, they were beyond the world view I had at the time. The stark reductionism of Monica's observation merely shocked me. I was not capable of understanding that the universe as revealed by science can be viewed both reductively and holistically. Even if I had, I am sure I would have rejected it as the product of a cold, rational mind that I would always be opposed to. It was a long time before I came to see that science and art are not in opposition, but are concerned with the same thing — the scientist tries to understand the universe objectively, as far as is possible, through measurement; the artist looks at it subjectively through the eyes of humanity. Both ways of looking can be held in the mind at the same time and the one can enrich the other. *Pace* Keats and his rainbow, to look at the Black Mountains and appreciate their grandeur and beauty is not incompatible with knowing their geological composition and how they were formed from an eroded plateau that had once been laid down under the sea.

Drink

Alcohol was something I came to slowly and reluctantly. When I was eighteen or nineteen I preferred the Continental Café opposite the Town Hall to any of the pubs in town. I had had a taste of my father's beer one Christmas and found it disgusting. I didn't like the stinging aroma of whisky either, nor the all-male, smoky atmosphere of bars. In the Continental, for the price of a coffee, you could sit and talk all evening. The coffee was frothy and tasteless, served in opaque white glass cups with saucers, but that didn't matter; what mattered was the feeling of independence, of emerging adulthood, as you put your money on the counter, then went upstairs, perhaps with Tom and Roynon, to discuss free will, or the latest books we had been reading.

Even at university I avoided alcohol, but when I returned to Abergavenny at the end of the first term, I found that Tom and Roynon had outgrown coffee bars in Oxford and wanted to go to pubs instead. I resisted but they were insistent and in the end I gave way. So we went to the Hen and Chickens where the brothers drank beer and I tried cider. I didn't like the taste or the physical effect a couple of half pints had on me, but it was better than beer.

And that is how it was through most of my undergraduate years. At Birmingham University the basement bar in the Students' Union would be crowded at weekends, the floor awash with spilled beer, and sometimes the metal shutters were pulled down around the bar if things got too rowdy. I went there a few times but didn't stay to drink. Only once in those three years did I get drunk when I took a small bottle of whisky back to my digs. The drink warmed me at first, but gradually I began to sweat and feel dizzy and then an urgent need to be sick. I managed to get to the back door and kneeling in the concrete yard brought up everything in the drain. I thought I was going to die and felt I deserved it.

That ought to have put me off alcohol for life but it didn't. Gradually it became a habit, a companion to loneliness, a solvent for nervousness, an antidote to boredom at parties where I didn't want to be. I wonder how many barrels, especially of wine, I have drunk in a lifetime — how they would look stacked in a dimly-lit warehouse where a sparrow cheeps among rafters unable to find its way out through the broken pane.

Ruins

I have always been attracted to ruins. There were the castles for a start, especially Skenfrith, Grosmont and White Castles, strung along the border and within easy reach of Abergavenny by bicycle. I liked their red sandstone, eroded to grey by wind and rain, the battlements and towers — especially White Castle's, looking out on undulating fields and hedgerows and beyond to the faded blue of the Black Mountains. I knew little of their history even after I began research into the Middle Ages as a postgraduate. I was drawn to their atmosphere, a certain resonance with which I felt at home.

It was the ruined farms of the Black Mountains that I found most appealing. Walking up a steep rutted lane I would come upon an isolated building, a sheepfold perhaps, or a barn, its roof of stone fallen in, the wood of its rafters rotten and gone. A wall might have collapsed, a jumble of stones with thick coats of moss. Always there would be nettles, and sometimes a sheep or two startled into flight at my appearance. The wind tugged at these walls as it did the walls of the castles. It was a lonely world, as if those who had prised the stones from shallow quarries in the hillsides and raised the walls, had one day got up and gone, leaving nothing of themselves except the labour of their hands.

These ruins became identified in my mind with Wordsworth's poem 'Michael', and 'the straggling heap of unhewn stones', meant for a sheepfold the old man lacked the heart to build.

In 1981 I visited Lybster in Caithness where my paternal grandfather had grown up before making the long journey to the South Wales coalfield as a lad in the 1880s. His family had been crofters and after some enquiry, together with my cousins Geoff and Alan and my wife Helle, we found the croft where he had been born. It was a low stone building with the byre at one end and the living quarters at the other. Although abandoned as a dwelling years before, it must have been used for storage until quite recently; part of the roof was still thatched with clumps of turf where the rafters had not collapsed.

This is how it would have started when farms in the Black Mountains were let go during the agricultural crises of the nineteenth century, a roof stone slipping, a window frame rotting, a tinkle of breaking glass that nobody heard.

Bird Watching

I have watched birds since I was eleven or twelve, but have never been an amateur ornithologist like R.S. Thomas or my American friend John O'Connell with whom I went bird watching in Denmark and Southern Sweden in the early '70s. My interest has always been aesthetic, with brief periods when I toyed with a more serious approach, as when at the age of thirteen or fourteen I subscribed to *British Birds*, the monthly journal of record for ornithology. Watching the birds in our back yard, I noticed a starling in the seething mass that came down each morning to fight over breadcrumbs. It had a distinctly longer beak than the others. I observed it for several days and then, certain I had discovered something special, wrote to *British Birds*. I received a friendly reply from the Editor commending my attention to detail but gently pointing out that minor differences of this sort are common in every species and to be expected. I didn't realise it at the time, but I had been given my first lesson in Darwinian variation.

I would go with a cheap pair of binoculars, a field guide and a notebook up the Little Skirrid or the Deri, or along the banks of the Usk or Gavenny to see what I could see. There was a rich variety, green woodpeckers, ravens, lapwings, curlews, long-tailed tits, dippers, common sandpipers, whitethroats, bullfinches, wheatears, whinchats and stonechats. But try as I might on occasion to be the hard-headed scientific type, it was always their beauty that won out — that quick glimpse of a green woodpecker's undulating flight between oak trees in Saint David's

Vale, with just time to absorb the wonderful emerald green of its plumage.

Often I would go for a walk without binoculars and field guide, taking pleasure in what I could see and identify with the naked eye. I'm in that phase now, as I write, walking from Comins Coch to Aberystwyth, watching hedgerow birds dart out of my path, a red kite hovering low over a field then veering away as it sees me. Few birds are indifferent to the advancing figure of a man.

Leaving

In 1958 it was time to try for a place at university. Wyn wanted me to sit the scholarship exam at his old college, Aberystwyth, and this I did. So one day in January or February 1959 my mother packed a small brown cardboard suitcase and I caught the train from Monmouth Road Station travelling up to Hereford through England to Shrewsbury, from where I caught the train for Aberystwyth.

It was dark and stormy as the train began its descent through the Cambrian Mountains. Engines were still steam-driven of course, and carriages compartmentalised with a connecting corridor running down one side. I was alone in my compartment and feeling lonely so far away from home. Suddenly the door slid open and the ticket collector stood there. 'Coast?' he enquired in a strong Welsh accent. I knew Aberystwyth was on the coast so I nodded.

The train reached Machynlleth and there was a short delay. Then it started off again. Sometimes the study of Geography is useful. After a while, glancing out of the window, I noticed that the sea was on our left. From the map of Wales I had in my head I knew it should be on the right if the train was going to Aberystwyth. I puzzled about this for a while, then in a panic it dawned on me that I was somehow on the wrong train. When the ticket collector, a different one this time, came round I explained to him my fears and he confirmed them. I should have changed at Machynlleth for Aberystwyth — 'Coast' meant up the coast to Pwllheli, everyone knew that, he seemed to imply.

He advised me to get off at the next station, wait for the down train to Machynlleth, change there, and travel on to Aberystwyth, as I should have done in the first place. I don't know where I got off — it was little more than a halt in what was now the darkness of a winter evening. There was no one else. I was alone with the immensity of the black sky and the rain and the wind.

After a long time a train came rattling out of the night and I got on, explaining to yet another ticket collector what had happened. I made sure I got off at Machynlleth and after another long wait eventually caught a train to Aberystwyth. I should have arrived late in the afternoon, but it was past 10.00pm when I walked out of the station into the town.

I knew that the hall of residence where I was to stay was on the sea front and I suppose I must have asked the way of someone who pointed me in the direction of Terrace Road. There was a hard wind blowing with gusts of rain, but when I reached the corner by the old King's Hall I was hit with the full force of a gale that almost snatched my suitcase out of my hand. It was hard to move against the buffeting of the wind; spray and shingle were thrown onto the Promenade with every wave that crashed against the sea wall.

When I reached the hall of residence, I must have registered, but I only remember entering a common room where there were half a dozen other scholarship contenders, all dark haired in my memory of them and all speaking Welsh together. So I sat there for a while by myself and then went to bed. It was too late to get a meal.

The exams and interviews lasted a couple of days. I have forgotten everything about them except that they took place in the Old College where the English

Department was still located. The interview itself was in a small room at the top of a circular staircase. There must have been three or maybe four lecturers crowded into it, one with his feet up on the mantelpiece. I remember nothing of what was said, only the tableau of three or four men trying to look relaxed — to put me at my ease, I suppose — but failing to do so in the confined space of the room.

My only other memory is of striking up an acquaintance with another boy from down Carmarthen way. We discovered we had a mutual interest in poetry and with nowhere to go in the evenings we discussed our favourite poets hunched in doorways out of the wind. I remembered his name because it was unusual, Byron Rogers. I didn't get offered a scholarship but Byron, I found out many years later, did. Had I been successful, I suppose I would have gone to Aberystwyth and my life would have been very different. At the time, I think I was relieved. The whole experience had been depressing and made me decide to take the unusual step of doing a third year in sixth form. The ostensible reason was to improve my grades at A-level, but it also meant a year's respite from venturing beyond the security of Abergavenny and the Black Mountains, and another year with Monica.

I had one other memory of Aberystwyth. Once in the early 1950s my mother and father decided that instead of going to Barry or Porthcawl for the day, as we did most Sundays in summer, we would go to Aberystwyth. This was a momentous decision for my father and I can't imagine what possessed him to venture so far. But we set off in our black Standard 12 full of expectation until somewhere near Nant-yr-Arian the car started to behave oddly. My father pulled over, examined the back wheels, and came to

111

the conclusion that one of the springs had broken. We drove slowly on, and when we reached Aberystwyth, instead of going to the beach we wandered around looking for a garage.

Aberystwyth in 1953 or '54 was a closed town on Sundays — nothing was open except the chapels. I don't know how my father did it, but somehow he found the owner of a garage in Cambrian Place, where Charlie's Stores are now, and persuaded him to look at the car. He confirmed that the spring had snapped and said he would make a temporary one which ought to get us home. My memory is of a dour, unfriendly man, but since we had taken him away from his day off perhaps that was understandable. He was almost certainly a Welsh-speaker too, while we spoke only English.

I know we sat on the beach, disappointed by its grit and gravel as opposed to the sand we had expected and I seem to remember the day as grey and dull. That could of course have been a psychological grey caused by worry over the car, or it could have been how it was since Aberystwyth is overcast most of the year. It took the mechanic all afternoon to make and fit the spring, and we left the town with a sense of relief, driving back through Mid Wales in the dark. We never went to Aberystwyth again.

The safe haven of a third year in sixth form passed quickly and in the New Year of 1960 I began the process of applying to universities all over again. This time I filled in application forms for Birmingham, Bristol, and perhaps Durham. Birmingham called me for interview, and again I set off by train, changing in Worcester and arriving at Birmingham Snow Hill. 'Snow Hill' is a name a bit like 'Greenland', the exact opposite of what it was. As my train approached the station, tall smoke-blackened walls crowded against the carriage windows with one or two weeds leaning out of cracks trying to catch the sun.

The two days of exams and interviews took place in the English Department's building in the centre of the city just before the Humanities moved out to the expanding campus in Edgbaston. I had arranged for a bed & breakfast nearby, and wonder now how I did that since my parents did not have a phone. Perhaps the University sent a list of B&Bs and I wrote to one of them.

As with Aberystwyth, I have only a glimmer of the two days that were to determine the course of my life for the next decade. There is Derek Brewer, the Chaucer scholar, invigilating one of the exams in a racing-green corduroy suit, walking up and down the aisles between the desks with what later always seemed to me an ironic smile. A pair of corduroy trousers was suspect in Abergavenny. A whole suit and in racing-green was unthinkable, yet here everyone appeared to consider it normal.

Then there was my interview with, I think, Elsie Duncan-Jones, the Marvell scholar who also wrote the first book on Gerard Manley Hopkins, though I knew none of this at the time. To me she was a rather nondescript, quietly spoken middle-aged woman, the same age as my mother. She asked me what I had been reading lately. I had been reading D.H. Lawrence — probably *Women in Love*, or *Sons and Lovers* — so she asked me what I thought of it and of Lawrence generally. I can't remember what I said.

At some point, perhaps on the last day, or in a break between exams, I had a browse in a second-hand bookshop and bought a copy of *Murder in the Cathedral*. It was a hardback with a classic Faber dust wrapper of the period where the design is in the lettering. I got it, I see, for 3s 6d as against the cover price of 7s 6d. Eliot's poetry, especially the poetry up to and including *The Waste Land*, already meant a great deal to me and this was a real find. There were no second-hand bookshops in Abergavenny.

Sometime later I must have received a letter offering me a place. It would have been a big moment yet I remember nothing about it. Perhaps it was an outright offer, perhaps it was provisional on improving my A-level grades in English and History. That, as it happened, would not have been a problem. When the results were due our doorbell rang and there was Wyn Binding. He had cycled round from school on the drop-handlebar bike he rode to and from Llanellen to tell me I had an A in English and a B in History.

Or am I misremembering? Had he cycled round the year before to tell me I had a B in English? The only thing I am certain of is my surprise at opening the front door and seeing Wyn in his cycle clips keen to tell me the news.

The more I try to remember the more treacherous memory seems to be. I have the programme for the King Henry VIII Grammar School Annual Speech Day held on Thursday, 17 November 1960 at 3.00pm. In it are listed the A-level results where it says I had a distinction in English, something I do not remember. I also won the English Prize and I do remember being asked by Wyn to choose a book. I chose Yeats's *Autobiographies*.

What surprises me more than anything, though, is that the address was given by 'R.H. Williams, Esq., M.A., Extra mural lecturer at the University of Oxford'. The Chair was taken by 'G.H. Tranter, Esq., J.P., Chairman of the Governors'. So there was Raymond Williams, disguised as 'R.H. Williams', rubbing shoulders with Mr Tranter, one of the worthies of the town, and with Colonel Edwards, the Headmaster. The Pandy boy and Rustican who had made good.

In November 1960 I was in my first term at Birmingham. Would I have come back to collect my prize in person? The course at Birmingham was so intensive and demanding that it seems unlikely.

1960 was the year Raymond Williams published his autobiographical novel *Border Country*, the book which made me realise for the first time that Abergavenny and the Black Mountains might be somewhere you could write about. If I was at the Speech Day in 1960 the name R.H. Williams would have meant nothing to me, however, because I did not read *Border Country* until 1962; he would have been a remote adult on the dais in the gym where Speech Days were held. But the more I think about it I am sure I was not there.

Later I discovered Raymond Williams had been with an anti-tank regiment in the Guards Armoured Division during the Second World War, involved in taking the bridge at Nijmegen while my cousin Bernard Howes was at Arnhem nearby where he was badly wounded in the head. Bernard went on to manage the science division of Blackwells in Oxford at about the time Raymond was R.H. Williams, extra-mural lecturer at the University — the one from Pandy, the other from Monmouth. I wonder if they would have had anything to say to each other had they met.

I lost my O and A-level certificates long ago but what I remember of the grammar school is my unrelenting mediocrity. I have one of my school reports for the summer term, 1954, when I was in second form. The form master was Wyn Binding who signed the report in his characteristic hand, 'FW Binding, B.A.', the F inverted so it looks like a Continental 7. For a time I started writing Fs like that, because it was Wyn.

I note that I had an A for conduct and was never absent or late — like the good shopkeeper's son I was — but came fifteenth out of thirty-three in class. This is reflected in my grades. In 9 subjects I was in the 50s and low 60s. My best grade was 74 for French; my worst 18 for Algebra, the latter a sign of things to come. The column for 'Teacher's Remarks' is somewhat anomalous — 55 for English (not taught by Wyn at this level) is described as 'fairly good', as is 53 for Latin, but Arithmetic (53) and Science (51) are considered 'good'. General progress was noted as 'good'.

And so it went on for my eight years at King Henry's. I was only ever in detention once when I was in sixth form for doing something I no longer remember. I do remember the humiliation, though, because detention for sixth formers was very rare. Trevor Evans, Physics, was taking detention that day and he knew my parents. He was a quietly spoken man and called me up to the master's desk. 'I'm sorry to see you here, John,' he said and asked me what I'd done. I told him and he nodded. 'Well get on with some homework then.'

Fifteenth out of thirty-three was the highest I ever achieved. The top positions were an unobtainable distance away and I could only guess what it would be like to come second or third. Perhaps that is why Wyn took the unusual step of coming to the house to tell me my A-level result. Perhaps he had been pleasantly surprised; yet there had never been any question that I should at least try for a university place, mediocre or not.

116

And of course Birmingham did offer me a place, rather to my surprise in retrospect, because though it was a 'redbrick' and considered second rate if you went to Oxbridge, the English Department happened to be one of the best in Britain at the time. When I was an undergraduate Derek Brewer, Geoffrey Shepherd, E.G. Stanley, David Lodge, Stanley Wells, T.J.B. Spencer, Elsie Duncan-Jones and I.A. Shapiro were all on the staff — leading scholars in their fields in the 1960s, while David Lodge was a much discussed novelist. Working the buses from Pontypool to Brecon that summer, absorbed in the sun and shadows of the hills, playing tennis and going out with Monica, I had no inkling of this.

Part Two

The Trunk

In September 1960 I finished on the Western Welsh and made preparations for my first term at university. There were set texts to order, Klaeber's edition of *Beowulf* proving a particular challenge to W.H. Smith's. When it finally came, in its sombre brown covers, I was intrigued by the Old English text of which I barely understood a word, and by the cramped scholarly apparatus which seemed just as impenetrable. One day, though, when I went to say goodbye to Wyn at his home in Llanellen, he took down his copy of Sweet's *Anglo-Saxon Reader* from the shelves. Don't be put off by Old English, he told me, there is some wonderful poetry in it, and he read a few lines perhaps from *Beowulf*, perhaps from *The Battle of Maldon*. I understood nothing of the words, but as with *The Waste Land*, it didn't matter — the music of the poetry came through and I fell in love with Old English alliterative verse.

But there were also more practical things to arrange. My clothes and other necessities had to be transported to Birmingham. My father owned a car but it never occurred to my parents or me that he might drive me there. That sort of thing wasn't done. You went to university by train, everyone knew that.

So my mother bought a trunk from Richards the Ironmongers. It was made of wood covered in reddish brown 'leatherette', with hoops of wood nailed to the outside as strengtheners. By the time it was filled it took two of us to lift it, and arrangements were made for it to be collected and sent as rail freight to Birmingham Snow Hill where

British Road Services were supposed to deliver it to my digs at 92, May Lane, Kings Heath.

My paternal grandfather, John Henderson Barnie, owned such a trunk when he travelled from Caithness to Brynmawr in the early 1880s, never to return. I have it still, the only relic from the crofting side of my family. It too is made of wood, the corners strengthened with broad metal strips that look hand-forged, as do the nails, perhaps by the village blacksmith, though the lock and handles must have been bought. It is taller but not as long as my trunk had been and is heavy even when empty. I believe he was eighteen when he left home; I was nineteen.

As the train steamed past the Mardy and Pandy I watched the hills recede — the Deri, the Sugar Loaf, Bryn Arw, the Big Skirrid. Finally there was the last dark scarp of the Black Mountains standing out like a defiance against the countryside of Herefordshire. At Pontrilas it was over, we were out of my area, and I sat back with a sense of loss that has never left me. Ten weeks later when I returned home for Christmas I leaned forward eagerly after the train left Hereford — there was the scarp at last, growing and growing across the fields, and then the Big Skirrid, Bryn Arw. As the train braked and slowed, there was the Blorenge, the Sugar Loaf, the Deri, the Llanwenarth Breast, the Rholben, and huddled below them the town.

But every leave-taking made me feel desolate. This was not helped by my mother who liked having the house full again and who long before it was time to go would say 'Oh, only two weeks left! If only you didn't have to leave!' She said it in a way I never fully understood, as if teasingly, almost with a hint of irony — though that is not quite right. It was as if she enjoyed the anticipation of sadness at parting and wanted me to share it with her. But I was only too aware that soon I would have to leave and I hated this, it was a kind of torture. Had we been an articulate family I might have discussed it with her, but I know she would have denied there was anything behind her put-on sadness. Perhaps there wasn't, but her wheedling made me burn with anger and frustration at times. Worst of all was the parting at the station. Monica and I would have kissed passionately the night before and my father gave me a good handshake with a smile, but my mother was always in tears.

That first time, I travelled to Birmingham on the Sunday before term started. When I got out at Snow Hill, the streets were deserted with that empty Sunday feel of post-war years. I had no idea where Kings Heath was or what bus would take me there, so I took a taxi.

May Lane — another of those lying names like 'Greenland' — turned out to be a narrow street of terrace houses built at the end of the nineteenth century. The taxi stopped at 92 and I got out with my suitcase and knocked on the door. My next sentence was going to be 'It was opened by my landlady...' The truth however is that it would be a narrative convenience because I have no memory of who opened it, though I do remember my landlady and her husband, a couple perhaps in their early thirties who had a daughter of about ten.

I remember my room, too. It was the downstairs front room, with a settee that folded out into a bed up against the window, a table and chair against the same wall as the door, and a dark varnished wardrobe against the wall facing the window. Opposite the door was a gas fire which had a meter into which you slotted half crowns or two shilling pieces, twisting a key so the coins fell with a chink among the cash already in the box. I was to have breakfast with the family, as well as an evening meal at, I think I remember, 6 o' clock.

It was probably the landlady who showed me into the room and when she had gone I unpacked my suitcase and looked around. I felt oppressed.

My trunk should have been delivered before I arrived but there was no sign of it. There was no phone so I had to go back to the railway station. I made enquiries and was taken into a storeroom piled with suitcases and trunks. I identified mine and was told it would be delivered next day, which it was, as I discovered when I got back from the university for dinner. I started unpacking but when I opened the door of the wardrobe I had a shock — standing amid the jangle of cheap wire coat hangers was the daughter. She jumped out and rushed from the room. I hadn't expected it. There was no lock to the door of my room and I realised I could not stop anyone from walking in.

During my first term there was still a lot of building work going on at the Edgbaston campus; the approach to the new Humanities bloc was muddy and lectures were constantly interrupted by pneumatic drills. I must have been given a timetable for lectures, seminars and tutorials. There were half a dozen lectures a week, seminars in Old and Early Middle English and possibly the eighteenth century, and tutorials on the Elizabethan and Jacobean periods. The student-teacher ratio in tutorials was three to one which I knew was inferior to Oxford where Tom and Roynon had one to one tutorials. My tutor, whose name I forget, was a specialist in the Elizabethan period, the other students in my group were a

Canadian woman whose name I also forget and Peter C—.

From the beginning I was out of my depth. The Canadian was an MA student who had been assigned to a first year tutorial group in order to achieve parity between her Canadian BA and an English one. She was therefore about three or four years older than me and had already done a degree. Peter C— was from Chester and had gone to Chester Grammar School. I soon learned the difference between a high-powered city grammar school and a country one like mine. Apart from A-level set texts, I had read unsystematically — Dostoyevsky, Kafka, E.M. Forster, Dylan Thomas, Wilfred Owen, Herman Hesse, T.S. Eliot — whoever I discovered or Wyn recommended. I'm glad I did this, but the contrast with Peter C— could not have been greater. Knowing what the first year syllabus was to be at Birmingham, his English master at Chester Grammar had set him an intensive reading course in the Elizabethan and Jacobean dramatists, so Peter was already familiar with the greater part of the tutorial programme before he came.

By contrast, I knew the two Shakespeare plays I had studied at A-level and had a passing acquaintance with a few others from sixth form trips to Stratford. There had also been the High School for Girls' overly ambitious production of *Macbeth* in which Monica played Malcolm. Some of the girls had had flour put in their hair to make them look like aged courtiers. They wore Viking helmets with horns and when at one point they had to take them off with a flourish the flour rose in a dust cloud around their heads. Monica was wearing a very short tunic and the only other thing I remember about the performance is her legs.

Tutorials were organised around the reading of an essay — it might be on revenge tragedy — which was then used as the basis for discussion. On average you had to read three essays a term. If I was not reading an essay I don't think I said much because I was overawed by the articulacy of the others. Once, when discussing *King Lear*, Peter C— said in an intense way, 'I think the only analogy to *Lear* is Beethoven's last quartets.' I had read *King Lear* for the first time that week and Beethoven was only a name to me. 'Fuzzy' Thomas, Woodwork, who liked classical music, had been assigned to teach us something about it in General Studies and he may have played a Beethoven symphony one dreary afternoon but it was not 'Rock Island Line' and it had gone over my head. So I was deeply impressed by Peter C—'s remark, which I concluded must be true because the tutor agreed with it.

In recent years I have come to appreciate classical music and I play Beethoven's last quartets often. I can see no analogy between them and *King Lear*, however, and I am inclined to think I was taken in by an act of cleverness. Wyn would have slapped me down for a remark like that, or if he thought there might be something to it, made me justify it. I had never encountered a delight in cleverness for its own sake, just as I had never encountered anyone who argued a position he didn't believe in.

Some years later when Peter and I were both postgraduates at the Shakespeare Institute, I took part in an informal study group where we read papers on whatever subjects we were currently interested in. I had been learning Old Icelandic and had become absorbed in the Greenland sagas and the extraordinary achievement of the early Norse voyagers in sailing across the Atlantic. I gave a paper

on this. In the discussion afterwards, Peter C—
demolished my argument, suggesting that the voyages
and the discovery of Vínland amounted to no more
than an historical sideshow. We had been friends for
some time and I was caught off guard by what felt
like a personal attack. I tried to defend myself but
became confused and inarticulate.

To my astonishment Peter then came to my
rescue, giving an eloquent defence of the Greenland
sagas and the Norse discovery of America. He had
only been playing with the opposite view, he told me
afterwards. This is what you learn in debating
societies and no doubt there was one at Chester
Grammar School. At King Henry's we had been
taught by Wyn to argue fiercely for positions we
believed in — nothing else would do. I couldn't help
being hurt by what Peter did; to me it was an act of
betrayal. I don't think he ever understood this,
however. He had put up a proposition for debate and
I had been free to refute it. When I failed to do so he
had come up with the counter-argument himself.
Where was the problem?

Once, the Canadian woman, who was married,
said of her father-in-law — in a context I have
forgotten — that he read widely and was a particular
admirer of E.M. Forster, but that if you asked him
what he liked about Forster's novels he was unable to
tell you. The tutorial group agreed that such
inarticulacy was deplorable, so I said nothing, but
secretly I didn't see why he should analyse his
reactions to literature in the way we were doing.
Wasn't the experience in itself enough? Secretly, too, I
thought the unknown, unseen man in Canada was a
bit like me.

I have a letter from my mother headed 'Sunday'
and date stamped 2 October 1960, so it was written at

the very beginning of my first term. 'Dear John,' she writes,

I expect you have settled in by now. Has your trunk arrived? You have probably discovered that I packed Michael's [my brother's] plastic mac instead of yours. I will send yours on & you can return his with your washing.

Your glasses have arrived at Kents but you will have to collect them yourself as Mr Kent likes to fit them & see that they are alright. He won't let Michael have them.

It is still raining here but not so cold. It looks as if John Lloyd [a school friend] is marooned in Exeter. I had to come home from the shop on Friday afternoon with flu, but feel much better today.

Michael didn't go to church this morning, he said four of the choir were on strike because Mrs Savagar had been very rude to Christine. He has just gone to Monica's for a maths lesson. Poor Monica, she has let herself in for something.

How did you get on at University? Let us know when you write. I expect you will soon find your way about.

If you have to dry anything in front of your gas fire, don't put it too near or you will scorch it.

It is very quiet here without you, only one record player going but it is on from morning till night.

They have delivered the Observer so I will post it on to you.

I am going to have a bath & then lie down for an hour.

I hope you have a good time with Tom.

If there is anything you want let me know.

Love.

Mum Dad & Mick

I would have been glad to receive this with its news of home. It reminds me now of things I had forgotten — that in sixth form I took *The Observer* on Sundays; that Tom Collings had passed through

Birmingham and I had seen him briefly. Then there are the things I half-remember like the dirty washing I posted home each week, receiving a parcel of clean clothes in return. This only stopped a year later when my new landlady, Pam Stefanovic, offered to wash my stuff with her family's. Why did I have my clothes sent back and forth in this way? It would have been difficult to dry wet clothes in my digs, but were there no laundrettes in 1960? There were certainly none in Abergavenny so perhaps even if they did exist we didn't know about them and my mother came to this arrangement.

The letter shows a mother ranging over potential worries — had my trunk arrived? — be careful with the gas fire — was I settling in? — there was difficulty getting my glasses from Kent's.

I knew intuitively it was not a good idea to confide in my mother, so I am certain that in my weekly letter home that first term I said nothing about feeling unhappy or out of my depth at University. As the days shortened through November and December, however, I became increasingly depressed by my digs with its weak overhead light, shabby furniture, and a gas fire that ate up the silver coins I slotted into it.

One evening as I sat there trying to work, there was a knock at the door and a fellow lodger, a second or third year student at the University, came in. I hardly ever saw him as he didn't have his evening meal at the digs and usually came home quite late at night. After some preliminaries he came to the point — he was short and could I lend him £5. He needed to pay the rent. He would pay me back as soon as his grant cheque arrived. I had the money so I gave it him and he left. Almost immediately our landlady came in and asked point blank whether he had tried to borrow money off me. I said he had and she told me not to do that again as he was completely untrustworthy, not to say a sponger. I couldn't afford to lose £5 but he was true to his word and a few days later returned the money. It confirmed a feeling I have always had — despite my parents' motto of 'neither a borrower nor a lender be' — that it was best to trust people until they let you down.

By the end of November it had become very cold. I couldn't afford to keep the gas fire on after I went to bed, and in any case it wouldn't have occurred to me — there was no heat in the bedrooms in Abergavenny. It was common to open the curtains in the morning and find the window panes covered with fern-like patterns of frost on the inside. But at home I had an old-fashioned feather mattress, plenty of blankets and an eiderdown, so I was never cold.

In May Lane I only had a sheet and a couple of blankets. As the nights got colder and colder I woke up freezing in the blank hours before dawn. I was too young and naive to ask my landlady for more blankets, though I suspect she had already given me all that were available. So I began wearing trousers and a sweater over my pyjamas, and in the end my duffle coat with the hood up as well. That way I could sleep, but each grey Birmingham dawn dragged me back to a world I survived in by withdrawing into myself. I know it is a gross exaggeration but looking back I seemed to inhabit a shadow version of the student Razumov's life in *Under Western Eyes* before he was overtaken by catastrophe.

After several weeks I got up courage to go and see the Accommodation Warden to ask if I could change digs. He or she, I can't remember which, was reluctant. Student accommodation was scarce. Why did I want to change? Shouldn't I try it for a while longer, at least until the end of term? Reluctantly I went away.

But I was lucky. Apart from Peter C— the only person whose acquaintance I made during the first term was Reinhard H—, an exchange student from Erlangen University near Nürnberg. I can't remember how we met up. It is highly unlikely that I would have approached him. One day I talked to him about the problems I had with my room. A few days later he said he had mentioned this to his landlady and that after consulting with her husband they had agreed I could move in with them in the New Year. It would be a tight squeeze because apart from Reinhard who had the downstairs front room, they had twins, a girl and a boy, who were perhaps three or four years old. The twins, it was decided, could move in with their parents and I could have their room. It would only be for six months because at the end of the summer term Reinhard was off back to Erlangen. I was pleased and relieved, and when the Spring Term began in January 1961, instead of returning to 92 May Lane, I packed my trunk and had it sent to 53 Midland Road in Kings Norton.

Old English

We learned Old English from Sweet's *Anglo-Saxon Primer*. Once a week about twelve of us would sit round a table with E.G. Stanley and he would examine us in whatever aspect of grammar had been set the previous week. Then we translated in turn from a passage in Sweet's *Anglo-Saxon Reader*, beginning with the easier prose passages from *The Anglo-Saxon Chronicle*. None of us much liked these classes. Stanley was an historical linguist and though this may be unfair to him, I don't recall him showing any interest in what we read as literature. But Old English was compulsory. There was an exam at the end of the first year, and if you failed you were not allowed to continue with Honours English.

I have never been good at foreign language grammar, especially the grammar of dead languages like Latin and Old English, so I tried to learn enough by rote to get me through the end of year exam. I faked it essentially, like 11-plus maths, and got through.

In the second year Geoffrey Shepherd took over from Stanley and we began a reading of *Beowulf*. It must have been about this time that I came under Shepherd's influence. He was a gaunt balding man with a sallow complexion and very bad teeth. I learned later that he had fought as an infantryman in Burma and there was a rumour that his indifferent health and poor teeth were a result of that experience. I never found out if it was true. I got to know him better when he supervised my PhD thesis, but he never mentioned his war experience.

Geoffrey was not a very inspiring lecturer. I remember him standing at the lectern in a suit and gown droning on rather like a downside-up bat. In seminars he was very different, quietly spoken and approachable, displaying immense learning as we laboured each week at the translation of *Beowulf* but in such a way that we were drawn deeper into the poem and never felt overawed. I enjoyed the *Beowulf* seminars so much that when in the third year we had a choice between continuing with Old English or opting for a course in early twentieth-century literature, I chose Old English. In the second year we had read half of *Beowulf* and I wanted to finish it — I was deeply attracted to the sonorous rhythms and dark music of this epic full of shadows:

Oft Scyld Scefing   sceapena preatum,
monegum mægþum   meodosetla ofteah,
egsode eorlas,   syððan ærest wearð
feascaft funden;   he þæs frofre gebad,
weox under wolcnum   weorðmyndum þah,
oð þæt him æghwylc   ymbsittendra
ofer hronrade   hyran scolde,
gomban gyldan;   þæt wæs god cyning!

I must have spent hundreds of hours reading this poem as a student and later on when I taught it at Copenhagen University, so that although I have not looked at it for some time I feel it is part of the furniture of my mind. When we came to study Middle English I was to feel the same about *Sir Gawain and the Green Knight*. Old and Middle English alliterative verse with its heavily stressed, alliterated lines taps into the music of the English language in a way that is more profound than poetry influenced by Renaissance obsession with a metrics derived from classical Latin, or so it seems to me. And alliterative poetry has never entirely gone away. It is there in disguised form in much of Shakespeare and more clearly in the poetry of Gerard Manley Hopkins and Ted Hughes.

What I never considered in my undergraduate years is that I was studying a course at an English university that was taking me deeper into the culture of England and further away from that of Wales. Had I won the scholarship and gone to Aberystwyth I would have studied an identical course taught mostly by English academics, but in a town that was one of the centres of Welsh-language culture. How might that have worked out? Might I have tried to learn Welsh far earlier than I eventually did in Copenhagen in the mid-1970s? Or would I have embedded myself in an entirely English cultural matrix as many people do at Aberystwyth University today?

It is impossible to provide an answer because when I was nineteen or twenty I didn't think of my nationality, I thought only in terms of five square miles around Abergavenny that was my home. Travelling to the Valleys, or deeper into Welsh-speaking Wales to visit Wyn after he became a lecturer at Trinity College, Carmarthen, was to enter an unfamiliar world, as was living in Birmingham where, although I never expressed it to myself, I knew I could never belong. If I fancied myself as an 'outsider' in Abergavenny, it seemed that I was doubly so wherever else I went.

Only after I moved to Copenhagen where I was confronted with a very different language culture that I couldn't ignore did I begin to ask questions about identity, and inadequately enough, to learn Welsh.

Germany

Reinhard was the first foreigner I got to know well. It is true that in Priory Road in Abergavenny there was an old lady who was rumoured to be French and that once when I was about thirteen I was asked to go over to her house to meet a niece who was spending the summer there. The niece, who *was* French, raised her right hand and presented the back of it to be kissed. That was not something you did in Abergavenny, and I don't think I understood what the gesture meant; at any rate I didn't kiss it. Then when I was in fourth or fifth form, a French boy joined our class for a term. I suspect he came from Paris though I have no evidence other than that he was quick-witted and a master pickpocket. Standing around in the playground with a group of us, he would suddenly produce a pen or wallet he had lifted without any of us noticing. When he gave it back he had an air of sneering triumph, as if we were country town naïfs on whom his talents were wasted.

With Reinhard it was different. We met at the university on a daily basis, and shared digs for the last two terms of his year abroad. He spoke good English and we got along, though the differences between us were profound. Reinhard was two years older than me; he had travelled in Europe and by the end of the year had hitch-hiked around Britain; he studied French as well as English, and was going to become a gymnasium teacher. I spoke no other language, had not been anywhere, and had no idea what I wanted to be.

There was another difference. In 1960 the Second World War was only fifteen years in the past. As a nineteen or twenty-year-old that seemed a long time ago, but of course it wasn't. Writing now, in 2012, the war would have ended in 1997 which is very recent indeed.

With Reinhard I gained a perspective on the war that was different from the insular one I had learned at home. His mother had worked as a secretary in the Reichskanzlei in the 1930s, before marrying. During the war his father had been a lieutenant in the Wehrmacht, fighting in the Balkans. In 1945, as the allies advanced into Germany, Frau H— took her four sons into the countryside to avoid the American bombing of Nürnberg. They were lucky, as was Hr H — who survived the war and, after undergoing a process of denazification, returned to practise law in the city, rising to be a judge.

The war was something that had to be negotiated. Late one afternoon, on the top deck of a bus as we returned to Midland Road from the university, Reinhard said reflectively that 'to some extent the Jews had brought it on themselves'. I was too young to stop and ask what he meant by this, otherwise I might have learnt something interesting. Instead I became passionate and outraged. The extermination of the Jews — I don't think I knew the term 'holocaust' then — was not something you discussed in shades of grey. Reinhard had no sympathy whatever with Nazism though I think he was conservative or at least became so as the years went by.

He was also deeply anti-Communist which was again something new to me. I had never met a Communist or thought much about them. From an Abergavenny perspective they were somewhere else a long way away and had nothing to do with our small-town world.

For Reinhard it was different. His country was divided, half of it in the grip of a Communist dictatorship. The blockade of Berlin and the Berlin airlift had happened only twelve years previously. I remember seeing black-and-white Pathé News footage in the cinema in Abergavenny with plane after plane taking supplies into West Berlin and the strident, clipped militaristic tones of the voice-over's narration. But emerging from the dark of the Coliseum or the Pavilion onto the familiar streets of the town, with the sun shining, and the green bulk of the hills all around, what had that to do with me? So I didn't understand when Reinhard said vehemently that during the 1956 Hungary uprising he had wanted to volunteer to go and fight the Communists in Budapest. I had seen Pathé News footage of that too — rubble-strewn streets, Soviet tanks grinding past ruined buildings, gun turrets swivelling menacingly, while men in civilian clothes clutching Second World War rifles peered cautiously round the corners of buildings or ran stooping in the grey blur of a catastrophe — images that became familiar as the twentieth century turned into the twenty-first.

Reinhard and I kept in touch after he left Birmingham and at the end of my second year he invited me to stay at his parents' flat in Nürnberg. So in the summer of 1962 I made the long journey to southern Germany by channel ferry and train. It was my first time abroad and as the train made its way along the Rhein valley I was surprised by the castles on precipitous crags that seemed intact and even lived in. The only castles I knew were Welsh and English ones that had been in ruins for centuries. The great Renaissance fortifications of Nürnberg were even more of a surprise; I had never seen a walled city.

It was also a discovery, though of course it shouldn't have been, that the Rhein was a working river with massive barges making their way north and south. It made the Usk look like the stream it was.

Reinhard lived with his parents in an apartment on Schwannstrasse from where he commuted to nearby Erlangen University. Everything was new to me — feather duvets, the whining sound of early morning trams in the street, the food, the voices, different perceptions of politeness, even living in flats. No one I knew lived in a flat.

In Nürnberg in 1962 you couldn't avoid the war. As we drove around the city Reinhard pointed out a large grey building still pock-marked from bullets or shrapnel. That was the SS barracks, he said. Later we went out to the parade ground where the Nürnberg rallies had been held. It was vast beyond my conceiving, with weeds growing between the concrete slabs. We got up on the dais with its brutalist architecture where Hitler had stood and made his raving speeches to rank on rank of human automatons below.

The war existed not only in its material ruins. One evening Reinhard produced a documentary LP about the Nazis which included excerpts from Hitler's speeches and the 'Horst Wessel Lied' sung with gusto perhaps by the Sturmabteilung. It was an extremely hot Middle European summer evening and we had the windows wide open with the 'Horst Wessel Lied' blaring out onto Schwannstrasse. Suddenly Hr H— came rushing into the room. He was a short man with stiff, swept back grey hair and a gruff voice. Frau H— could speak no English so we did a lot of smiling at each other. Hr H— spoke a broken English which he tried out on me when we met in the evenings. He was always kind to me, but this evening he was in a temper. I could not understand what he said but his meaning was clear. Reinhard was ordered to take the record off *at once*. What would the neighbours think, a high court judge listening to Nazi anthems and speeches, reliving the glory days? When Reinhard explained what Hr H— had said, I could see his point.

And there were Germans and Austrians who thought like that. Once, on a later visit, Reinhard and I were drinking in a Viennese Weinstube. At the next table a man perhaps in his fifties was talking earnestly with a companion. Reinhard was listening and I asked what the man was saying. He explained in a low voice that our neighbour was a Grossdeutscher who wanted Germany restored to its pre-war borders starting with the return of Sudetenland and East Prussia. He was a handsome man with a lean aristocratic appearance typical of photographs of Wehrmacht and SS officers I had seen.

Much later, in the 1990s, Reinhard began sending me newspaper cuttings about the millions of Germans who had to abandon their homes as the Soviet army advanced. There were cuttings too about allied atrocities. Stories of families travelling to Poland after the fall of the Soviet Union to knock on doors of houses and farms where they or their parents had lived half a century before. He rarely commented on them in his letters but I understood the message.

I met one family of refugees in 1962. Reinhard was engaged to Hildegard and we went to visit her parents in nearby Wilhermsdorf. They had an apartment in what had been a small Schloss in the centre of the village. The Schloss itself was run-down with certain original features that I had never seen before. The toilet consisted of a raised wooden platform with a round hole in the middle covered by a wooden lid. When you raised the lid there was a rush of ammonia from rotting fæces and urine that took the breath away and suspicious gurgling sounds from somewhere far below. It was not a place to linger. You did what you had to, put the lid back on and cleared out holding your breath.

The apartment had the high ceilings and plaster moulding of the eighteenth and nineteenth centuries and the rooms echoed at footfalls and voices. It was a relic of a vanished world, and now it housed Hr and Frau Lumplesch on its first floor. Before the war they had been farmers — peasant farmers I would think — somewhere to the east, possibly in East Prussia though I cannot be sure. When it was clear that it was all over and Soviet forces were driving deeper and deeper into Germany, Hr Lumplesch abandoned his farm and took to the road with his wife and daughters, moving ever west to avoid the revenge of the Russians. Reinhard told me they had passed farm after farm where cows stood in the fields lowing painfully for the burden of milk in their udders. But the farms were deserted and there was no one to milk them. Hr Lumplesch was a very tall, gentle man, not at all like the stocky Franconians I had got to know through Reinhard. He sat there on our visit with his hands hanging over his knees. They were large, powerful hands, but it was as if they were fashioned for a different life and he had no use for them any more. It had grieved him to pass those farms, to walk on in the growing line of refugees, knowing he could do nothing for the animals that were hurting.

In the 1960s I made a number of visits to Nürnberg, a city I grew to like, but after I moved to Copenhagen in 1969 the visits gradually ceased. During the '70s summer and Christmas vacations were spent back in Abergavenny. I still met Reinhard occasionally, twice in Copenhagen, and we corresponded. In 2003, however, another war caused a final breach between us. It became clear that, come what may, George W. Bush was going to invade Iraq and I became deeply angry as did many others in Wales at the lies we were being told, at the overbearing arrogance and sneering cruelty of Bush, Cheney and Rumsfeld, and at the posturing and mendacity of Tony Blair, their sanctimonious 'ally'.

Reinhard saw things differently, however, and for the last time the Second World War overshadowed us. As a German he was grateful to America. The Marshall Plan had helped West Germany to emerge from its ruin. Now that America was in trouble — he was thinking of the destruction of the World Trade Center and the threat of Al Qaeda — it was the duty of her friends to rally round and support any action she saw fit to take. The problem for me was that Iraq had nothing to do with Al Qaeda or with the 9/11 plot. The invasion was a war of aggression fought on blatantly trumped up grounds. What was the duty of America's friends? To support her, right or wrong, or speak the truth, no matter how unpalatable that truth might be? Reinhard and I argued this back and forth in letters, until in one letter he told me that it didn't matter anyway what a little country like Wales thought about world events. From that moment the relationship faltered and eventually petered out.

Long before this, in the summer of 1961, the Second World War had also come between Reinhard and our landlord Radomir Stefanovic. Although it was a tight squeeze at 53 Midland Road, my impression had been that we all got along, but just when Reinhard was due to return to Germany, Radomir had a fierce row with him. I wasn't there and never really discovered what it was about. Reinhard was hurt and puzzled. All Radomir would tell me later was that he thought he could put the war behind him but found he could not.

Reading

The Honours English course at Birmingham was intensive and involved a lot of reading. If the tutorial group was studying Milton you would be expected to read *Paradise Lost* and *Paradise Regained* in a week. If it was Wordsworth, then it was *Lyrical Ballads* and *The Prelude*. On top of this, every third week you had to write the tutorial essay. That was only the core. There were also thirty or forty lines of *Beowulf* to translate and absorb for the Old English seminar, and perhaps a few pages of *Ancrene Wisse* for Middle English. In the third year there was a Victorian seminar taught by a very young David Lodge. I believe it was his first job and he came armed with a folder of notes. George Eliot might be the subject, in which case we were expected to read at least *The Mill on the Floss* and *Middlemarch*, also in a week. Even as a self-absorbed student I felt sorry for David Lodge. Reading for tutorials had to take first place, and by the time we came to his seminar many of us were at the limits of what we could absorb. The result was silence around the table with Lodge forced to answer his own questions. He needed those notes. Later, as a young lecturer at Copenhagen University I had the same experience and doubly sympathised with him as the minute hand crawled painfully round the face of the clock.

My problem was that I was a slow reader, so I was forced to spend all my time reading. After breakfast at the Stefanovices I caught a bus to the university and if I didn't have a seminar or a lecture went straight to the library. I set myself a strict routine. A cup of coffee in the campus café at 10.30, lunch (usually a fried egg in a bap) at 1.00, another coffee at 3.00, and dinner in the refectory at 6.00. During these breaks I would meet up with Peter C— for a chat. Then it was off to a seminar or lecture or back to the library. The café, refectory, library and English Department were on three sides of the campus green which was more than convenient. After dinner I stayed at the library until it closed at 9.30, sometimes cat-napping with my head in my arms on the desk.

At weekends I didn't go to the university but worked in my room. Occasionally I would take a Saturday evening off if Radomir suggested going to see a film. One evening we saw Marcel Camus's *Orfeo negre* which transposes the myth of Orpheus and Eurydice to Rio de Janeiro in carnival time. As a twenty-year-old I was overwhelmed. I have never seen it since but certain scenes have stayed with me — the colour and vibrancy of the carnival, Euridyce waking at dawn, her long hair spread artfully over the pillow, Death in tight-fitting black clothes with the bones of a skeleton stencilled over his arms and legs and torso, and the bones of a skull hiding his face as he hunts Euridyce through the carnival crowd. Radomir and I discussed it on the way home. He agreed that it was good but said it was a 'young man's film'. My head was full of the beauty of Euridyce, Death's silent prowling as he tracks her down and corners her in a deserted factory, Orpheus's desperate attempt to save her, and me knowing the story and that it cannot be. So I was annoyed when he said it was a young man's film. Now that I am older than Radomir was in 1961 I can see that he was right. Perhaps it is why I have never made an attempt to see it again. It would be too much to be abused of my first experience — to see from the outside what I had so passionately seen from within.

When I was a teenager and in my twenties I often reacted in this way. One evening I went with Tom and Roynon to see Sydney Poitier in *A Raisin in the Sun* about a poor black family who come into insurance money and move into a white suburb in the hope of bettering themselves, only to face a wall of white hostility and racism. As we filed out of the Pavilion and walked up the Hereford Road I felt deeply moved by it. I didn't see how anyone could think differently, but Tom and Roynon did. It was all right, they said, but nothing special. *A Raisin in the Sun* is another film I have never seen since. I am sure, still, that *Orfeo negre* is a great film, but Tom and Roynon were probably right about *A Raisin in the Sun*. I was always letting emotion get in the way of judgement, always setting up heroes.

Reading so intensively to a programme for three years had a bad effect on me. In sixth form I had read what I wanted outside the A-level syllabus and had immersed myself in the experience that Lawrence or Kafka had to offer. But there was no time for this at university if I had to read *Tom Jones* and *Pamela* in a week and perhaps write a tutorial essay on them as well. So I came to depend on criticism as a short cut, and at a certain level I think this inhibited my ability to think. 'Too much Hough' was scrawled at the bottom of one essay by my tutor when I had relied too heavily on Graham Hough's little book, *The Romantic Poets*, and he was of course right, but given the intense demands of the syllabus and my own slowness there was very little else I could do. After the finals exams in 1963 I felt burnt out and it was a long time before I was able to read for pleasure again. When I became a lecturer at Copenhagen University I was forced into another relentless course-driven programme of reading. Then too I read and absorbed criticism, but since I finished teaching I have hardly done so at all. In fact I have developed an antipathy to literary criticism. This is not because I have become so arrogant that I think there might not be something to learn, but because I no longer wish to have a poem or novel mediated for me through the thoughts of others.

At Birmingham I would go on reading after I returned to 53 Midland Road at ten in the evening, but there I often had an unwelcome distraction in the form of my landlady Pam Stefanovic. Pam was a Londoner with a strong Cockney accent. She was younger than Radomir and I never discovered how they met after he came to England. Even as a twenty-year-old, however, I could see they were mismatched. Radomir would often retreat into a book, but Pam needed to relieve her frustrations by talking and often she turned to me. She would knock on the folding partition that created a narrow corridor to the front door, draw it back a little and stand there unburdening herself. This wouldn't have been so bad except she never knew when to stop, so I had to sit there patiently sometimes for an hour or more. I could of course have said 'I'm terribly sorry, Pam, but I really have to get on with this reading', but I have always found putting people off difficult, so I never did. Instead I raged at her inside my head, inwardly shaking with anger and frustration because she couldn't see I needed to work. Eventually she ran out of steam and said goodnight, but I was usually too angry by then to get back to what I had been studying.

Peter C—

I never went home during term time, but Peter C— did, to see his long-time girlfriend, his cousin Ann. Once or twice he invited me along to stay at his parents' and somehow I found time to take a weekend off.

When I first met him in 1960, Peter was a natty dresser with a neutral educated English accent. You knew he was grammar school and would probably place his parents in one of those 1930s semi's with faux half-timbering and a neat front lawn hedged with laurel.

When I went to Chester for the first time, therefore, I was surprised. Peter's parents lived in the middle of a row of nineteenth-century back-to-backs with front doors opening directly onto the street. It was one among dozens of streets all looking the same. This placed Peter C—, the Chester Grammar School boy who could leap from *King Lear* to Beethoven, who sported a tightly furled umbrella and usually wore a three-piece suit, in a new light. His father and mother were short and portly and had Cheshire accents. Mr C— was an electrician and wore a cloth cap. He was inventive and in the days when tape recorders were expensive had built one for Peter from scratch. It was a reel-to-reel, large and very heavy. Peter's mother was like so many mothers of my acquaintance who always seemed to have an apron on with a halter neck and strings tied in a bow at the back. You would usually find them in the kitchen, or hoovering, or cleaning the windows. They may have had jobs as girls but once married the home became their work and their world.

Mr and Mrs C— were warm and friendly. There was no side to them, even if from an Abergavenny point of view they had some strange ways, like insisting I take a very large glass of orangeade to bed in case I 'got thirsty in the night'. I explained that I didn't think it likely, but Yes, they insisted, you never know.

There was a disjunction between the Peter C— I knew at university and the one who grew up in this tiny terraced house. Peter was an only child and his parents were proud of him, but I found it hard to say what his attitude to his background was. He rarely referred to it in Birmingham, any more I suppose than I referred to Abergavenny. Our relationship was contained within the artificial world of the university. I only recall him mentioning Chester once when in our first-year tutorial we had somehow got onto the subject of immigration and racism. The tutor said he thought racism was endemic in Britain. Peter disagreed. If an Indian family moved into his street in Chester people would welcome it, the women in their saris would add a bit of colour. I had no opinion on this. When I visited his parents, though, I recall the street being one hundred percent white. In 1960 Peter's optimistic view of Chester's working class had yet to be tested.

In 1965 or '66 he got a lecturing post at Exeter University and I used to visit him and Ann there. At first they lived in a small modern house on an estate, but later moved to a two-storey Edwardian house in town. In the early '70s Mr and Mrs C— were on a visit at this house when Peter had a serious quarrel with his father who accused him, more or less directly, of betraying his class.

That scene must have been enacted many times as clever grammar school boys got educated out of their parents' milieu. When I was a postgraduate studying at the Shakespeare Institute in Edgbaston Park Road there was a fellow student who was the son of a Durham train driver. He had a somewhat plummier accent than Peter. He and his father were no longer on speaking terms.

I never found out whether the row between Peter and his father led to a permanent breach because in 1976 I quarrelled with him myself. We were in a restaurant in Exeter when the subject turned to Welsh nationalism. I had been living in Copenhagen for seven years and had gone through a process of rethinking what identity and nationality meant. I was teaching myself to read Welsh and was reading Kate Roberts, D.J. Williams and T.H. Parry Williams with the aid of a dictionary, as well as rereading R.S. with different eyes. Coming from Chester, Peter and Ann had often visited North Wales and had that familiar English view of it — Wales was a wonderful place with such beautiful scenery and a delightful language, but it could never be anything other than a part of Britain. Welsh nationalist aspirations were absurd and irrelevant to the modern world. We had been drinking and most of my quarrels have occurred when drink has lowered my petit-bourgeois inhibitions. I became intensely angry at what seemed to me their boundless English self-confidence and arrogance and I lost my temper completely.

The next morning my wife Helle and I were due to catch the train from Exeter to Abergavenny. Peter came with us to the station and we stood on the platform in silence until the train pulled in.

In a way, the quarrel was no surprise. There were times when we were very close as undergraduates, and when I returned to Birmingham in 1964 to study for an MA Peter and Ann often invited me to stay over on Saturday nights in the guest room at the old people's home where Ann was Matron and where they had a flat. This was in the outer suburbs and involved a long bus ride to the terminus. The home was part of a vast new council estate which already seemed run-down even though it was new. There was one pub — I don't think there were any shops. Ann's flat was on the first floor of the home and looked out on a large playing field where no one ever played. It was just a bare parade ground of grass.

The home was mostly inhabited by old ladies who seemed jolly enough. Ann would tell how on her rounds one would say to her, 'Oh, Matron, look — I've lost a toe in the night!' holding it up and laughing. Once, in summer, a sudden gust of wind blew a garden parasol past the flat's windows to hoots of laughter from the old ladies below who had been sitting in its shade around a table.

Once, too, as we leafed through the Sunday papers, I thought I heard bagpipe music. This seemed so unlikely that I went on reading. It persisted, however, so we went to the window and there was a piper in full regalia playing a lament, as he walked slowly round the perimeter of the field. It was the most beautiful thing in this unlovely world of municipal planning. When he reached the side opposite the home, the piper left through a gap in the railings. We never saw him again.

Those were the good times, but Peter had a northern Englishman's sharp tongue and a way of passing off barbs as wit, like the woman I overheard in Sheffield talking about a bad meal she'd had in a Manchester fish restaurant. 'The chips 'ad eyes in 'em — they could see where they were going. So I said, "Well we're not paying for this", and as we were walking out the manager shouted, "Hey, I want to see thee", and I said, "Aye, I want to see thee an' all. We come from bloody Sheffield, we're not bloody stupid".'

This kind of bluntness is hard to deal with if you come from the Welsh border where people conceal their feelings and avoid confrontation. What is verbal sparring to a northerner looks more like naked aggression to a borderer, and I was never sure how to respond to Peter's barbs, because I didn't know, and still don't know, how far he was merely being witty at my expense and how far he was expressing his frustration and annoyance at my slowness or obtuseness. 'Small hath continuous plodders ever won,' he said once, meaning me. I was hurt, but I also knew it was true. I *was* a plodder, just about holding my own in the English Department, term by term.

A break with Peter was inevitable. When it came I was upset but partly because yet again I had repressed my feelings only to have them burst out in uncontrollable anger. I never tried to make contact after the quarrel and recently I saw on the internet that he died in 2011.

Back Home

At the end of the first term I was keen to get back to Abergavenny, to work as a Christmas postman, to live at home again after ten weeks in May Lane, to escape the alienation I felt as I got off the bus each day and walked to the university. Above all I would have wanted to get back to Monica. She was in second year sixth form by then and in the autumn of 1961 would be going to teacher training college at Retford in Nottinghamshire.

Thinking about it, I can't be sure what our relationship was. In 1960 she was seventeen. Girls of that age now seem to slide in and out of knowingness and innocence but to me then she was a fully formed woman whose body I longed for night and day. No wonder her father kept a sharp eye on us when we were round at her house.

If you came from a small town like Abergavenny, though, passion was continually frustrated by chasteness. I think Monica was as sexually charged as I was, but there was always that threshold that could never be crossed before marriage. And I suppose in one way it was a good thing. Contraceptives were unobtainable if you were a teenager in Abergavenny. Where would I have gone? To Shackletons the Chemists? But Mr and Mrs Shackleton lived just across the road from us and Mrs Shackleton was my mother's best friend. To get a girl pregnant was unthinkable. When it happened to the girlfriend of someone I knew at school, it was hushed up. The girl was taken out of school and sent away to have the baby who was put up for adoption.

So sex was always on my mind and we made passionate love that was never consummated. After my finals in 1963 Monica and I went to Spain with her friend Maureen and Maureen's boyfriend. We had hired a holiday chalet with two bedrooms with single beds. Monica and Maureen shared one room and Maureen's boyfriend and I the other. Driving through the Pyrenees on the way back, we stopped overnight at a hotel in Andorra where they only had available one room with single beds and one double. Monica and I volunteered to share the double and Maureen and her boyfriend took the singles. I remember Maureen being shocked that we could be so daring. She was clearly glad it wasn't her, though I don't recall the boyfriend expressing an opinion. I wanted at least to make love as far as we usually did but Monica must have thought it too much of a risk and we just lay there all night side by side.

Despite frustration piled on frustration, it was good to be with her again that Christmas, yearning for the feel of her body, burning up with Lawrentian desire. If *Orfeo negre* was a young man's film, Lawrence's novels were a young man's fiction, though I didn't think so at the time.

I can't remember if it snowed that vacation but if it did I would have taken at least one walk in the hills, following the path through Saint Mary's Vale and along the Rholben, or up over the face of the Deri and along its ridge to the Sugar Loaf. After a hard climb there would have been the whole world spread before me, snow white and milky grey, and silent except for wind snagging on exposed rocks of the summit. That was to be home again.

Pessimism for Beginners

Everyone who knows me would probably agree I am a terrible pessimist and I have often wondered how I became that way. Are pessimists made or born? My father was a pessimist. 'That's a bad 'un', he'd say when we played snooker in the Conservative Club, and he'd say it before the cue ball hit the colour as if to confirm his own estimate that he was a poor player. Other members of my family were pessimists too, usually the males.

Perhaps it is impossible to disentangle a genetically inherited trait here from the influence of environment; perhaps the former is merely reinforced by the latter. In my case there is another factor, depression. Since at least my teenage years my moods have oscillated between highs and lows. These swings, I know, are related to the writing of poetry.

My sense of this was confirmed from observing my younger brother who in his early twenties was afflicted by the onset of manic-depression. He wanted to be a painter and studied at Newport School of Art. Manic-depression, however, destroyed his ability. When he was manic he had huge ideas, there was no limit to what he was going to do. But that was at the beginning of the upward curve. As his mind raced faster and faster he lost control, the projects became grotesque and beyond his reach. Then suddenly they all collapsed and he fell headlong into a deep depression, often phoning to say he wanted to kill himself. Drugs controlled these swings except in periods when he refused to take them, but the drugs made him passive, blanking out the creative urge.

I have long noticed that my own swings between high and low are similar but less violent and destructive. The upward swing, if I am lucky, releases a poem. At times I will sit down every morning for days or weeks just to see if anything is there, but a poem cannot be forced, it will come when it is ready.

There is truth to the ancient idea that poetry and madness are allied. My brother, who died in 2007, was the dark mirror to my own mind.

Is my innate pessimism therefore a function of a biochemical oscillation which creates a filter through which I interpret the world, knowing that every high must be followed by a low? And do eternal optimists have the reverse perception, because every low must be followed by a high?

It is hard not to reflect on this because people prefer to be in the company of optimists. Yet if habitual pessimism distorts reality, so does habitual optimism. In 1938 it was right to take a pessimistic view on whether a devastating European war could be averted. Today it is hard to see how coming generations are going to cope with human over-population and the problems it is causing — depletion of resources, mass extinction of species, global warming, among others.

Perhaps, though, it is the optimists we must look to if solutions are to be found. My pessimism inclines me to become an observer of processes which seem ineluctable because humankind has reached the limit of its ability to organise for the common good. My preferred philosophy, if you can call it that, is Robinson Jeffers' Inhumanism. Perhaps I am wrong.

Radomir

Although I didn't realise it at the time, an important part of my education was taking place outside the university at 53 Midland Road thanks to my Serb landlord, Radomir Stefanovic.

The English couldn't get on with a name like 'Radomir' so everyone called him Steve including his wife, and I suppose I must have done so as well. Here, however, I prefer to call him Radomir.

He was tall and handsome, with the slightly heavy features of a certain kind of Serb, not unlike Radovan Karadzic. When I first knew him in 1961 he must have been about fifty years old. Before the war he had trained as an architect but his qualifications were not recognised in Britain so he was forced to take whatever job he could get. When I knew him he worked as a wages clerk at Cadbury's in Bournville. Radomir was an intelligent man and the work was tedious and routine and poorly paid, but he had lied about his age even to get that. Jobs for refugees with heavy foreign accents, limited English, and no paper qualifications were not so easy to come by in post-war Britain.

I am not sure why he ended up in Birmingham — he had met Pam in London — but it may have been because there was a significant Serb community there. Pam didn't speak Serbian and I don't think she made any attempt to learn it. She did have a Yugoslav cookery book though, and on Sundays would cook various Serb dishes which seemed very exotic to me. Radomir also had a coffee grinder made of brass with elaborate scrollwork that made it look 'eastern' and I think it must have been at 53 Midland Road that I first tasted real coffee. At home we always drank Nescafé. Sometimes Pam even obtained green coffee beans, something I have never seen since, and roasted them herself.

The Serb community in Birmingham kept in touch with one another especially on national feast days. Once I went with Radomir, Pam and the twins to Sveti Slava, the celebration of family patron saints, at the Serbian Orthodox Church. This was an Edwardian suburban house and on the outside didn't look like a church at all. Inside, however, a large room had been converted into a piece of Serbia. I was used to low-church St Mary's in Abergavenny, with its grey stone walls and grey pillars reaching up into the gloom; even the air seemed grey. The Serbian church however was all light and gold. There were dozens and dozens of candles, gilt everywhere, and icons of doe-eyed Eastern saints in gilt frames. The priest was splendidly robed in contrast to Canon Davies's grim black and white, and had a huge beard.

The women, including Pam, had brought offerings of bread plaited in intricate patterns, and there were delicacies like poppy-seed cake. There was a service with hymns that were very different from the ones I was used to. I used to feel depressed when the Canon announced, 'We will now sing Hymn One-hundred-and-thirty-two. One-hundred-and-thirty-two', and the organ cranked out the melody to a clearing of voices and a collective rustle when the congregation stood up, as if reluctantly, to sing. These Serbs sang with great emotion. There was an aura of melancholy in their voices, or so it seemed to me, not understanding the words.

After the service the food that had been brought was laid out and the congregation split up into groups around the table. Poppy-seed cake seemed to me then, and now in memory, the most wonderful cake I have ever eaten.

At the time I probably resented being dragged away from my university studies. As one of the few monoglot English speakers present I would also have felt awkward and out of my depth. The experience has never left me, however. It was a glimpse of a brighter, more flamboyant, but also a more tragic religious world than the one I came from.

Now and then, in the evening, some of Radomir's fellow Serbs would gather at No. 53 — a dozen or so men who crammed themselves into the tiny living room at the back of the house. Many, I think, were ex-Chetniks, like Radomir himself. There was always a bottle of bootleg slivovitz which they drank out of tiny glasses, knocking the shots back in one. As the evening progressed a man I remember as slightly younger than the others would take out a piano-accordion and start to play. He was a brilliant musician, one of the finest I have ever heard. His fingers danced across the keys and buttons like butterflies as he played the traditional music of his people. Then the others put down their glasses, formed a circle, and with their arms over each other's shoulders performed a ring dance.

Once someone produced a cassette tape and the men gathered round a tape recorder to listen. It was a recording of a male-voice choir. They sang in what was to me an unfamiliar close harmony songs which I knew were songs of loss and mourning. The men listened intently and some had tears glistening in their eyes.

When they had gone, I asked Radomir what the songs had been about. He told me they were songs about Draza Mihailovic, the Chetnik general. Radomir had served under Mihailovic during the war, ending as a major I think. He sometimes talked about his war experience. His unit had fought against the Nazi invaders and against the partisans. The Chetniks had been betrayed by the British, he believed. At first, arms had been dropped to them as well as the partisans, but toward the end of the war Churchill decided to throw in his lot with Tito and air drops to the Chetniks stopped. The propaganda broadcasts continued, however, urging them to fight on.

When it was clear the war was ending and that afterward the partisans would be in control, Radomir took his men over the mountains into Italy. At times they were reduced to eating grass and many died on the way. They thought they would be safe in allied hands, but the British had made a deal with Tito and Radomir's men were herded into cattle trucks and shipped back to what was to become Yugoslavia. He never found out what happened to them, but many who were returned in that way were imprisoned and shot. Because he could speak Russian Radomir was sent by the British Army to Berlin to act as an interpreter. He remembered the ignorance of the Russian peasant soldiers. Many had wrist watches they had looted strapped up their arms. When one wound down and stopped they thought it was broken and threw it away.

In return for his work with the Army he was given refugee status and allowed to settle in England after the war. Twelve years or so later I got to know him. Radomir's father had been killed by the Germans in the First World War, his own life ruined by the Nazis in the Second. He was never able to go home even on a visit — as a former major in the Chetniks he knew he would be arrested and probably executed. After many years his mother was allowed a visa in the late 1960s to visit him in Birmingham. It was not a success. She only spoke Serbian and Pam who was thrown together with her all day while Radomir was at work, spoke only English. There were frictions of the expected kind and Radomir never saw her again.

The war in Europe seemed to follow me around. My cousin Donald Howes had been killed in Italy. My third year tutor, Derek Brewer, fought there, as did Huw Davies, art master at King Henry's. Huw had been a private, Derek an officer. Either might have been present when Radomir came down into Italy from the mountains. Reinhard's father, Hr H—, was an officer in the Nazi army occupying the Balkans. Had he and Radomir met, they would have tried to kill each other.

One evening as the party in the living room broke up I followed them to the front door on my way to my room. After they had gone Radomir turned toward me in the empty corridor and said something in Serbian. It took a moment for him to read my face, and then he switched to English.

Years later when I was living in Copenhagen I became a friend of Emanuel Halicz, a Pole from Lwów in what is now Western Ukraine. In 1941 Emanuel was studying History at Lwów University when a professor came into the lecture hall and announced that the Germans had broken through and would soon be in the city. He advised everyone to evacuate at once.

Emanuel knew by 1941 what was in store. He didn't go home to take leave of his parents but went straight to the station and caught the first train heading east. He eventually succeeded in crossing the border into Soviet Russia where for the time being he was safe. The Russians gave him work as a teacher in a provincial school in North Russia.

I was a baby in the safety of Abergavenny in 1941 while Emanuel, a twenty-year-old, was wrenched from everything he knew. I don't know if he ever saw his parents again. He never mentioned them and I wonder if they perished in the extermination camps.

Later, in I think 1943, he joined the Polish People's Army as a junior officer and took part in the Soviet offensive of 1944. In one battle, he told me, he was standing next to Wojciech Jaruzelski, a fellow officer, when Jaruzelski was wounded by shrapnel. Emanuel was surprised when he became Prime Minister in 1981. 'Little Wojciech, what have you done!' I remember him saying in Copenhagen.

Emanuel was there too in September 1944 when Stalin halted the Soviet advance on the banks of the Wista while the Germans crushed the Warsaw uprising and razed the city to the ground. He remembered the flames and the sky at night glowing red, and the feeling of helplessness.

He met his wife, Anna, after the war. She was a Polish Jew. She would have been a young woman when she was sent to a concentration camp by the Nazi occupiers. Somehow she survived. Anna never talked about this period in her life and I only know about it because Emanual told me once. I never asked for details.

In 1944 I would have been three-and-a-half. There are three faded Box Brownie photographs of me taken almost certainly that year — sitting astride a rocking horse in the yard; making mud pies; attempting to sweep leaves with a broom twice my size. In all of them the sun is shining.

Glimpses

Apart from going to a few of his lectures, I was never taught by I.A. Shapiro, but his lectures were memorable — not so much for their content, as for their asides. 'Is Miss Dunstan here this morning? Now Miss Dunstan you have a dentist's appointment at 12.30. Please do *not* forget it. There is nothing worse than neglecting your teeth.' In fact Shapiro's lectures were a bulletin board where any number of announcements might be made before he turned to his ostensible subject. He was a thin man with greying hair and a goatee beard and he talked very slowly and very precisely. It was rumoured that he had been working on an edition of John Donne's letters for many years and that when the typescript was almost finished it was stolen from the back seat of a car. I don't know whether it was true or not. Shapiro was very particular about details. His wife had a bad leg, and some years later when I was at the Shakespeare Institute, I would overhear him giving instructions to one of the secretaries who was to order theatre tickets for himself and Mrs Shapiro. 'Now please remember,' he would say, 'they have to be in rows five or six and with an aisle seat on the *left*' — so Mrs Shapiro could stick her leg out, presumably. I have always imagined him publishing notes on minutiae in *Notes & Queries*. He died in 2004 aged 99.

The philosopher Peter Geach was equally impossible to miss. Shapiro was finicky and dapper, but Geach in the early 1960s was large and shambling with greasy straggling hair and staring eyes. There are numerous stories about him and it may be that none of them are true. One concerns a young academic who stood staring at the lecture-hall blackboard which was covered in mathematical symbols. Peter Geach had been lecturing there just before him, proving (or disproving, I forget which) the existence of God. As the new man was about to wipe the board clean Geach's staring head appeared round the door — 'I forgot to say,' he announced to an entirely different set of students to the ones studying philosophy, '— there's a flaw in my argument.'

It was also told that he and his wife, the philosopher Elizabeth Anscombe, devised a unique way of potty training their children. They reasoned that if you carried a baby around in a brown-paper carrier bag, when it wet itself it would also wet the bottom of the bag upon which it would fall through. This would be an unpleasant experience for the baby and once it had happened four or five times it would learn that wetting itself was not a good idea. It's an interesting hypothesis but after they had tried the experiment a few times someone reported them to the RSPCC. Or so the story goes.

I never had cause to speak to Geach but I did talk now and then to Spencer Davies who was a year above me studying German. He caught my attention because I would sometimes see him carrying a twelve-string guitar around the Humanities building. Twelve-strings were uncommon — I don't think I had seen one before. So I asked him about it. Like me he was interested in the blues and had ambitions to form a rock group and become a professional musician. He was studying German on sufferance, or so I thought.

I don't think he had a Welsh accent because I had no idea he was from Swansea and he wouldn't have known I was from Abergavenny. I didn't move in his circle and we only chatted occasionally. He was the only Welsh person I ever met in Birmingham.

The truth though is that I didn't move in any circle. Once, probably in the second year, Peter C— and I quarrelled. I can't remember why. For several weeks we eyed each other in the Humanities building but did not speak. In my undergraduate years Peter C — *was* my 'circle', so for most of that term I ate by myself in the refectory and spoke to no one except Radomir and Pam. Eventually Peter approached me and the quarrel was patched up. I would not have done it.

Monica

By my second year Monica was at Retford doing teacher training. I wrote to my mother once a week out of duty. I wrote to Monica too and waited impatiently for her replies. I remember her coming to Birmingham on two occasions. Once we met at the Kardomah in the city centre. It was a basement café and dark but she insisted on wearing sunglasses like a film star. I suppose she thought it made her look mysterious but it annoyed me because while I was talking to her I couldn't see the expression in her eyes. I asked her to take them off but she refused, giving me the Mona Lisa smile. We were due to meet her parents and when they arrived, Mr Bennett, who was a brusque Nottinghamshire man, said something like 'Come on Monica, take those sunglasses off; stop acting daft', and without a word she obeyed.

Another time she stayed the weekend at No. 53. Radomir was a man of the world and wouldn't have minded had we slept together. When the Profumo scandal broke he said over and over in his heavy Serbian accent, 'Poor Mr Profumo. Poor Mr Profumo.' Why the fuss? What had he done? In Serbia, he explained, a politician would be *expected* to have a mistress. So, no, he wouldn't have minded had we slept together. I wouldn't have minded either but Old Abergavenny reached even into the suburbs of Birmingham. Monica was to have my room, while I slept upstairs. That Friday evening I reluctantly turned my back while she undressed and got into bed, then we kissed and said goodnight.

I kept her letters in bundles for many years in a drawer at home in Abergavenny. One day in the '80s, after I returned to Wales, I took some out with the intention of reading them. I started one. It was written from Retford in that round girlish hand I had known so well but I couldn't finish it. I was afraid, I think, of discovering a truth I did not wish to know — that the passionate intensity of our relationship as it exists in memory might be contradicted by the ordinariness of the letters.

Later I burned them in the garden.

Finals

Three years seem a long time when you are nineteen but the blink of an eye when you are older. In the spring of 1963 I had to prepare for my final exams. As I recall, there were nine three-hour papers crammed into just over a week. These covered the Victorians, the Romantics, the Eighteenth Century, the Seventeenth Century, Shakespeare and Elizabethan drama, Chaucer and Late Middle English, Early Middle English, *Beowulf* and Old English, and a paper in a subsidiary subject, which in my case was History. In the third year there had been a choice between Old English and Early Twentieth-Century Literature. As I have mentioned, I chose Old English but most of my contemporaries chose the Twentieth Century.

After the first two or three weeks of the summer term, teaching stopped and I decided to go home to revise. In the exams you were expected to quote from the poems or novels you answered questions on but were not allowed to take any texts into the examination room. This was a problem for me because I have never been able to remember quotations. Much of my revision took the form of deciding what aspects of, say, Pope, might come up on the Eighteenth Century paper, then rehearsing in my head suitable answers and memorising relevant quotations. I walked round the lawn in the back garden saying over and over Thy hand, great Anarch! lets the curtain fall; And Universal Darkness buries All; Thy hand, great Anarch!... Thy hand, great Anarch!... Thy hand, great Anarch! lets the curtain fall...

I walked round the lawn so much that after a couple of weeks I wore a distinct circle in the grass as if I were a prisoner in an exercise yard. The garden in summer was my father's pride but he didn't complain.

It was a poor way to revise, but I didn't know a better one. With three questions to answer on every exam paper there were dozens of quotations to remember. In the exam, too, there would be no time to think, so I had to have relevant thematic points fixed in my head. It would have been better to have *thought about* the authors I had chosen and to have done some selective rereading, but I was too slow for that. With an hour to answer each question I knew I had to seize on a topic and start writing straight away.

There is probably no satisfactory examination system. I am glad my degree involved a comprehensive study of English literature from the eighth to the twentieth centuries because it provided a foundation on which I have built ever since. However, the course impeded my ability to think in the way Wyn Binding had taught me. The opportunity was there and indeed it was expected of you, but the extent of reading required, combined with my own slowness, meant I battled for three years to keep up. In the process true thinking was set aside. As I discovered later, postgraduate research suited me better.

When it was time for the exams I took the train back to Birmingham. There followed an unreal ten days in which, apart from eating and sleeping, I did nothing but exams or last-minute revising for exams. If there was an afternoon without exams it was an opportunity for more memorising; when a weekend intervened before the last exams it was more revising morning, afternoon and evening. At the beginning of my third year the Stefanovices had moved to a larger house in Willow Avenue in Bearwood and I had moved with them. Peter C— also had digs in Bearwood or somewhere near, and on the Sunday afternoon we arranged to meet half way, but it was only for a few minutes, and only to ask each other how we were doing.

In one of the first exams a girl gave a moan and keeled over in a dead faint on the floor. Porters were called and she was carried out. The rest of us carried on. There was no sound except the rustle of a turning page, the scribbling of pens, and sometimes the footfall of the invigilator as he stretched his legs walking up and down an aisle. Afterward we emerged blinking into the sunlight, comparing notes.

It was as if we lived in a bell jar in which ten days stretched out endlessly because time had slowed down. Then suddenly it was over, the jar was lifted and we were out in the ordinary world, except it didn't seem ordinary, it seemed strange. It is how prisoners must feel when released from gaol. I was hollow and lifeless.

I could have gone home but I know I stayed in Birmingham a little longer because Peter C— and I would meet on the green in front of the Library where he introduced me to Harry Martinson's *Aniara* in a translation by Hugh MacDiarmid and Elspeth Harley Schubert. It had been broadcast as a serial on the Third Programme. Peter read passages from the copy he had bought and I was taken with it, so I went to the campus bookshop and bought a copy for myself. We also read Tolkien's *The Lord of the Rings* whose escapist fantasy suited my mood after finals. Many years later when Harry Martinson became a pivotal writer for me I returned to *Aniara*, reading it in Swedish. In the summer of exams, though, I read the great space epic with interest but then turned to something else.

Tom and Roynon had also been sitting finals at Oxford and we agreed to take a week's camping holiday in Scotland when they were finished. So eventually I left Birmingham, as I thought for good, and took the train back to Abergavenny. Mr Collings now owned a car and since Tom had recently passed his driving test, his father rather amazingly let him borrow it for our trip.

Despite being an ex-policeman, Mr Collings himself was an erratic driver. He always turned out of Woodland Road onto Park Crescent instead of the other way onto the Hereford Road. There was less traffic on the Crescent but it had the disadvantage of a hedge that completely blocked the view of any traffic coming from the right. Mr Collings would have his polished 99ers on the pedals, peering out to the right, revving the engine impatiently. One car would flash past, then another. *Revvv-revvv.* Eventually his patience wore thin — he was an irascible man at best. 'Here goes,' he would say as he launched the car into the unknown. I know this because Oxford terms were out of synch with mine and once or twice I went with him and Mrs Collings on a day trip to the 'Mecca of Learning'.

Mrs Collings would load the boot with homemade fruit cake in biscuit tins, a roast chicken, and other good things to keep up the brain-power of her boys. Mr Collings only bought petrol from Shell and though he would have tanked up in Abergavenny, every time we passed a Shell petrol station Mrs Collings would say, 'There's a Shell station, Ralph.' Silence. Trees, hedges, telegraph poles, farms, villages flashed by. Then 'There's a Shell station, Ralph'. And so it went all the way to Oxford.

Mr Collings was one of those drivers who is never in the wrong — being an ex-policeman might have helped — but he was often a menace. In particular, he never got the hang of roundabouts. He would simply nose into the circling traffic to an irritated tooting of car horns. From the back seat I could see his bull neck getting redder and redder as he shook his fist at a motorist or even wound down the window to give him a piece advice.

Tom, studying Mathematics, thrived at Oxford, as he had at Monmouth School for Boys where he had been Head Boy, but Roynon hated the school and the university. He was at St. Edmund's Hall — 'Teddy Hall' — a sporting college, full of rowing and rugby blues. Roynon liked sport but he hated the jockstraps and their crude behaviour. He didn't think much of his tutor either who lived in college. A morning tutorial was invariably held in the tutor's bedroom where the latter sat propped up in bed, sipping sherry while Roynon read his essay.

That was all behind him now. The Oxford results had been published just before we left for the Highlands, so Tom knew he had a First and Roynon an Upper Second. My results would come out while we were in Scotland, and I arranged to phone my parents on a certain evening to find out what they were. This is another example of fallible memory because if asked I would say my parents didn't get a phone until 1968 or '69. My father didn't see the point. When he had to make a business call, which was rare, he went next door and used the phone in his sister and brother-in-law's shop. If he wanted to talk to someone he went and knocked on their door. What do you want a phone for? Yet we must have had one in the house by 1963 because I know I phoned there from Scotland.

The journey North was uneventful except that Tom, a novice driver, backed the car into a ditch as he tried to do a U-turn on a single-track road in the Highlands. The car was heavy and the three of us couldn't lift it out, so we found a phone box and got hold of a garage that had a breakdown service. Eventually a Land Rover appeared, driven by a middle-aged Scot in a kilt. He didn't think much of us, for all kinds of reasons I should imagine. He fixed a towrope, hauled the car out, charged 10/- and drove away without saying a word.

We ended up in Skye, camping near the shore not far from the Cuillin Mountains. I had never seen white sand before and was surprised when I looked closely to see that it appeared to be made up of fragments of coral. I had never experienced the warm summer nights of the North either when light dwindled but never entirely disappeared. Even at midnight I could read a book, sitting by the glimmering sands.

That was one of the last times I went camping, an activity I have always disliked. When you can sit in a chair, eat at a table, and sleep in a bed in a house, why would anyone want to undergo the misery of lying on hard cold ground, worrying whether the tent will leak when it rains, trying to cook over a smoky fire? I know it is different now with every convenience you can think of packed in the car but as far as camping is concerned I have sympathy with John Tripp's 'Great Indoors'.

On the way back but still in the Highlands I made the phone call as arranged. We had stopped to camp near a small wood of Scots pines. It was evening, and while Tom and Roynon prepared the campfire I went to a phone box just down the road. It was probably my mother who answered the call but she put me on to Monica who was back from Retford and wanted to give me the exam results. At first she teased me, refusing to tell me what I'd got. With my small change running out I began to get irritated, but with fine timing she told me at last that I had a Lower Second.

In English at Birmingham in the early 1960s Firsts were rare and in some years not awarded at all, there was a narrow band of Upper Seconds and a few Thirds, but the largest band was Lower Second. Although I knew deep down that is what I would get, a feeling of intense disappointment stole over me and I went for a walk in the pine wood. The sun was mellow in the evening warmth and there was a glow to the reddish bark of the trees. A few birds must have flitted about in the canopies of the pines but I didn't notice.

Nottingham

During my undergraduate years I never thought of a career. As finals loomed, however, I couldn't avoid it and even before I got my results I had come to the conclusion there was nothing for it but to teach. Tom was going to study Theology at Wycliffe Hall in Oxford and Peter C— who got an Upper Second was staying on at Birmingham to do an MA. Like me Roynon could think of nothing better and with an Oxford friend of his, Henry Ferns, we applied for the one-year Diploma in Education at Nottingham University.

We were accepted and in October 1963 found digs in a run-down Victorian house close to the site of the annual Goose Fair. It was a two-storey boarding house run by the marvellously named Mrs Mountjoy and her middle-aged daughter. Mrs M. had a club foot which clumped at every other step as she led us up the stairs to the second floor where the three of us were to share two rooms. It was a cold-water flat, with a stone sink and a cold tap on the landing where we had to wash. The rooms were large but dingy. I think there must have been a bed or a bed-settee in the living room which we tossed for and which Roynon won. Henry and I shared the bedroom. This was bare except for two very old-fashioned brass bedsteads the springs of which pinged and twanged whenever one of us turned over. If you turned over too quickly the bed rolled on its castors in a stately manner across the slant of the floorboards.

The flat had one other feature. I had brought my Dansette record player from Abergavenny and after we dumped our belongings I plugged it in and put a record on. Nothing happened, then black greasy smoke started to coil from under the turntable. I leaped up and turned it off. Mrs Mountjoy had neglected to tell us the house was wired for DC not AC electricity. It must have been one of the last in Britain.

In the first week of the new term we were given a general introduction to the course then plunged straight into three weeks of teaching practice in a primary school. In my school I was assigned to a class of eight or nine-year-olds. The teacher, a man in his early thirties, was brilliant. Without raising his voice he got twenty or more boisterous children to settle down and become absorbed in whatever task he had set them. I watched him for a lesson then he handed over to me and left the room. In an instant there was chaos. Nobody would sit down or stop shouting and soon one boy was crying because a fat boy had jabbed his hand with a pencil. Why did you do that? I asked, trying psychology, but the fat boy wouldn't answer. The children had to bring pencils to the teacher's desk to be sharpened in an industrial-sized sharpener screwed to the desktop. You inserted a pencil and turned the handle. It looked simple but every time I removed a pencil the lead would be broken at the tip. So I inserted it again and turned the handle again as the pencil got shorter and shorter. Even when I succeeded the child would soon be back in the queue holding a blunt or a broken point. I was beginning to feel like Gulliver among the Lilliputians. Eventually the day ended and I went back to the flat. I seem to remember that Roynon's experience had been similar, though Henry, who was genial and easy-going, had done better.

After three weeks in which I failed to teach or keep order it was back to the Department of Education and the theoretical component of the course. We had to read Piaget on child psychology and an abridged version of Rousseau's *Émil*, but I can remember very little else about the course.

That November Kennedy was assassinated. Henry and I were sitting in our living room at the Mountjoys when Roynon, who had been visiting his girlfriend, came back with the news. We were deeply shocked because like everyone else we were taken in by the Kennedy myth. We had read *Animal Farm* and *1984* but made the common mistake of thinking they applied only to the dismal Communist states in the East. It took me a long time to realise that whatever their surface meaning these novels laid bare the mechanism of politics everywhere and that we were just as blinded and misinformed by the propaganda of the Americans as the other animals were by the pigs in *Animal Farm*.

The winter of 1963-64 was incredibly cold. When we returned to Nottingham after Christmas, Henry and I had to put on sweaters and trousers when we went to bed in the unheated bedroom. We piled our coats and anything else we could think of on top of the blankets but we were still cold. It snowed and the snow turned to slush and the slush to ice that stayed on the pavements for weeks. Henry had discovered Sylvia Plath's *The Colossus* and enthused about it. She had killed herself in the similarly harsh winter of 1962-63 though I'm not sure whether we knew that.

The term after Christmas was entirely given over to teaching practice when we had to spend ten weeks in a secondary school. I played safe and opted for a grammar school as did Henry, but Roynon in an idealistic mood chose a secondary modern and was allotted a school in a rough part of town. I was sent to the Brunt's Grammar School in Mansfield and had to get up about 6.00 in order to make a 7 o'clock bus to Mansfield, washing in cold water, snatching something for breakfast, then trudging through the freezing dark to the bus stop.

The Brunt's was a boys' grammar school like King Henry's only larger. The masters wore gowns so I had to bring my BA gown back from Abergavenny. I taught all classes from the First Form to the Sixth under the tutelage of the senior English master. I was lucky. He was like Wyn, enthusiastic about literature, very knowledgeable and a fine teacher. He kept an eye on me and gave me good advice. I particularly enjoyed teaching the eleven-year-olds and the Sixth Formers. But it was a huge strain. I didn't get back to the Mountjoys before 5.30 or 6.00 in the evening. It was dark when I left and dark when I returned and everywhere except in the school was cold. A quick meal and it was down to preparation and marking, early to bed, then up at 6.00 for another day of drudgery. There was one other pupil-teacher at the Brunts and sometimes he and I sneaked out at lunchtime for a pint of cider in a pub in town. I don't know what would have happened had we been found out.

At least I had no discipline problems. The boys at the Brunts were well behaved even in the third and fourth forms unlike at Roynon's secondary modern where he struggled to keep control and his idealism wore thin. He came back to the Mountjoys one afternoon with black ink stains spattered across the back of his corduroy jacket — his only jacket, I think — flicked there by pupils when his back was turned. It was ruined.

I was rapidly coming to the conclusion that teaching was not for me, and so was Henry. We stuck the course out, however, moving to a flat on the first floor of a semi in Lucknow Avenue and then to a terraced house in Florence Grove near a deserted railway yard. The terrace was old and run-down and due for demolition. There was little furniture but enough for us to squat there in the hot summer term of 1964.

At Lucknow Avenue I had my only experience of smog. The thaw came at last and one evening I walked out into an enveloping split-green-pea-coloured nothingness. A few steps and our house disappeared. If I stretched my arm out I could just see my hand. As I walked cautiously like a blind man a street lamp would appear emitting a mustardy light that spread a few feet above my head, illuminating nothing. There was no traffic — buses, cars, had ground to a halt. Ragged flakes of soot the size of old pennies drifted past or floated this way and that as if falling in suspension. I forget where I was going that evening but I knew there was a danger of getting lost. There was no landmark anywhere even though I knew there were houses all around with their lights on. One false step and I would quickly have no idea where I was and I think I must have turned back. Perhaps I had gone no further than a hundred yards. In the morning the smog had lifted and the city returned to the drab air of decayed nineteenth-century industrialism that I knew so well from Birmingham.

Retford was not far from Nottingham and sometimes on a Saturday I would take a bus there to spend the day with Monica at her teacher training college. It was an all-girls residential college and students were only supposed to have men in their

178

rooms if the curtains remained pulled back and the door was unlocked. Sex, it was made plain, was off-limits. Monica half obeyed these rules while I was visiting and half not, which meant that we half made love as in Abergavenny. Occasionally too she would come to Nottingham where we were freer, though not at Mrs Mountjoy's which had the dismal atmosphere of a back staircase in Gormenghast or one of the joyless dwellings in *The Secret Agent*.

The end of year exams approached and Roynon, Henry and I decided to turn what we had learned about 'group work' to our advantage. We divided the core themes of the course between ourselves and another student who joined us. Then we read up on our subject, reported back to the group and distributed a set of notes. It worked — we all got Upper Seconds.

The question was what to do next. Henry, whose parents were Canadian, was going to a university in Ontario to study for an MA and Roynon had secured a job in a comprehensive in Lincolnshire. I knew I was temperamentally unsuited to teaching. I had come into contact with two marvellous teachers during the year and I admired them, but their gift seemed to me instinctive rather than learned, and I knew I did not have that instinct.

I decided to see if I could go back to Birmingham to do research. I knew my BA was against me, but I wrote to T.J.B. Spencer, the head of the English Department. He replied that if I could fund myself the department would take me on for a two-year MA by thesis. I was still in love with the Middle Ages so I asked my third year tutor, the Chaucerian, Derek Brewer, whether he would supervise me. He agreed.

I must have discussed this by post with my parents and my father said he would lend me £300 which in 1964 was enough to live on for a year. It was a loan but he never asked me to pay it back.

Part Three

Writing

That summer I returned as usual to Abergavenny and it was then I had the idea of writing fiction; short stories perhaps. So I bought some paper and started writing at the kitchen table. That is how I remember it, except it cannot be true because another memory, a small detail, intervenes. I know I made clean copies of what I wrote on a portable typewriter and I didn't have one of those until well into the first year of my MA. I must have started writing later, perhaps in the summer of 1965.

What I wrote, however, didn't progress beyond a paragraph or two. Somehow I could never construct a plot. There was a scene or a character sketch, and that was it. I can see now that I was writing embryonic prose poems, but in 1964 or '65 I had no thought of writing poems, and since I appeared to be no good at fiction, I shelved the project, plunging into academic research instead. In the light of what happened in 1974 I regret that I didn't pursue the urge to write, but it may be that the urge was not strong enough. It is certain that it was misdirected toward fiction.

So began a period lasting ten years in which I considered myself a 'medievalist' becoming — two research degrees later — a lecturer in Old and Middle English literature at Copenhagen University.

Research

By agreement with Derek Brewer I was to write a thesis on the ideal of knighthood in fourteenth-century romance. To embark on such a project now would make me ill but when I was twenty-three it was exciting — discovering a whole world of literature, good and bad, that I hardly knew existed in the bound, sober editions of the Early English Text Society in the stacks of the University library.

At the end of the first term Derek wanted to see something in writing, so I handed in what I thought was a draft of the first chapter. It was rejected in a friendly but firm manner as stylistically inept, an undergraduate essay of the kind I had done for three years. I had to begin again. There was more to learn than I realised about the techniques of research, how to marshal an argument, and crucially how to present it in clear, concise prose.

When at the end of my first year Derek Brewer left to take up a fellowship at Emmanuel College, Cambridge, Geoffrey Shepherd agreed to take me on. His first comment on reading what I had written was 'Well, I wouldn't have approached it like this.' He didn't elaborate but because I admired Shepherd, the hint was sufficient. At the end of two years I had done enough to get an MA. I never looked at the thesis again.

Singleton & Cole

In the summer of 1965 the £300 my father had given me ran out so I had to find a way of financing myself. I can't remember now how I got the job but I began working at the tobacco wholesalers Singleton & Cole whose warehouse was in a run-down section of town not far from the Bull Ring, a criss-cross of streets occupied by small manufacturers and traders no doubt long since demolished. The company itself was not so small, however, as it supplied tobacco retailers throughout Birmingham and the Black Country.

My job was to make up the orders as they came in from tobacconists and corner shops. These were written on standard forms that sometimes arrived in twos and threes and at other times in bundles of forty or fifty. There were long rows of metal shelves piled high with boxes of cigarettes in cartons of 200, every kind of pipe tobacco, and a whole section devoted to snuff. I took a form and went up and down the aisles assembling the order — 800 Park Drive, 400 Craven A, 600 Benson & Hedges, 400 Players Navy Cut, 10 packets Old Holborn, 1 box menthol snuff. Occasionally there would be more exotic orders for Balkan Sobranie, or one of the specialist snuffs, or a box or two of cigars.

The cigars were kept in a special locked room and I had to get the key from the foreman, Fred. It was a dark, still room with an aroma all of its own, rich and velvety and somehow sweet. There were the flat boxes arranged on shelves, and boxes, too, of the most expensive cigars in slim metal tubes. I liked the boxes of Cuban cigars best with their romantic colourful labels depicting palm trees, elegant women and moustachioed men and the names of the company in elaborate scrolls in Spanish. I didn't have to go in there often but when I did I lingered as long as I dared — Fred kept a sharp eye on the key — breathing in the scent and examining the boxes. I was teaching myself Spanish at the time and liked reading the labels.

As I was making up an order I put the items on a long table running the length of the room. When it was complete the order form was placed on top and I told a checker on the other side of the table it was ready. These tables really formed squares with surfaces at right angles joined to another parallel set of tables so that when the items on my order form had been checked and ticked off, the checker could push them round to the table behind her where they were collected by one of the van drivers. There was a constant coming and going of vans with a roaring of engines and slamming of doors.

When a large bundle of orders came in we were very busy as they had to be made up immediately. At times though there would be a lull and then I sat around on the tables talking with the other assemblers and checkers most of whom were women. In 1965 everyone at S&C was white, working class, and Birmingham-born. That did not seem strange at all and was not the result of a racist policy — half a century ago Birmingham was still an overwhelmingly white city, though within a few years of course that would change.

Sometimes too when there were no orders I walked up and down the aisles looking at the exotics. There was a South African pipe tobacco called something like Uitspan which was sold in small sacks gathered and tied at the neck. Printed on the cotton was the bearded image of a Voortrekker and the company's name in Afrikaans. Through the cloth the strands of tobacco felt hard like nail clippings.

What I liked best was the snuff section which I sampled surreptitiously. Menthol snuff which we sold most of was like sniffing Vicks but then there were the specialty snuffs that came in small cylindrical tins with screw caps. My favourite was James Robertson Justice's No. 1, the name printed in delicate copperplate on a white label. It was dark as gunpowder and when I sniffed it there was a momentary explosion and startling clarity in the forepart of my brain.

I worked at S&C's five days a week from 8.30 a.m. till 2.30 p.m. then caught a bus to Edgbaston, writing up my thesis at the Shakespeare Institute till about 9.00 when I went for a pint at the Gun Barrels just below the University on the Bristol Road.

The Gun Barrels in the 1960s was a late Victorian pub with decorated tiles on the walls and several snugs. The clientele were a mix of Old Birmingham and students. At the back was a crown bowling green, the first I had ever seen as I don't think they exist in Wales, where a club of old age pensioners played in the summer. There was no friction between students and locals that I ever saw. If I was by myself I would go to the snug on the right where I usually sat, and take out a book and read. There were often other readers, including a mature student who someone told me was a 'White Russian', though I don't know if it was true. I watched him once as he sat ostentatiously on a stool speed reading, or pretending to. His eyes flicked from side to side, following his finger down one page then down the next, then in a flash over to the next opening. He gutted a three hundred page book in about ten minutes. Then he downed his drink and walked out while I returned to my slow plod through a Spanish novel. I wished I could read faster, but I didn't see any point in reading the way he apparently did.

I was frequently hungry in those days and with a pint might order a hot steak and kidney pie in a tinfoil container, or a pickled egg. At the warehouse we had a twenty-minute break at 10.30 when we all rushed up to the staff canteen for a cup of tea and a slice of white toast spread thick with margarine. The women all sprinkled salt on theirs and I started doing the same. It tasted good.

We ate at formica-topped tables but the management had a table to themselves which was set apart from the rest. When we went up for our break, it would already be laid for lunch with a white linen cloth and knives and forks and spoons. I rarely saw the managers — the warehouse looked after itself under Fred's care and they almost never came down to inspect us.

Fred had a wooden office rather like a sentry-box the walls of which were covered with notices. He was portly and had a problem with his feet which caused him to wear special bulbous-toed shoes in which he shuffled painfully around. Perhaps he had rheumatism or arthritis because he was unable to articulate his neck fully. He kept his chin down on his chest so when he wanted to look at you he had to lean back. Fred was a gentle man and a worrier. It was important for us assemblers that the shelves were constantly restocked. This applied particularly to popular brands like Park Drive which went out of the warehouse so fast they were left in boxes on the floor and we helped ourselves from there.

It was Kenny who was responsible for restocking from a storeroom at the far end of the assembly area. Kenny was young, had a shock of yellow hair that was in permanent disarray, and was not very bright. We would tell him if we were short of anything, and he would come lumbering along with the boxes piled on a trolley, tipping them off so they tumbled on the floor. This used to annoy Fred. 'Kenny!' he would remonstrate. 'What?' Frequently we would be out of Park Drive or Benson & Hedges and the assemblers would start shouting. 'Kenny, where's those Park Drive?' 'Come on Kenny!' 'Alright! Alright! I'm not a blinking slave.' But he was, in a way. There would be no better job in life for Kenny.

As when I worked on the Western Welsh, we were paid in cash on Friday afternoon. The brown packets with cellophane windows were brought down from Accounts and distributed by Fred from his sentry-box. We all gathered round and Fred peered through the cellophane and called out a name. For a few minutes there was silence as we opened our packets and counted out the money against the statement. Then Fred got restless, shooing us back to work.

Being paid in cash is much more satisfying than having your wages paid by cheque or directly into your bank account. There is something real about unfolding a bundle of notes, of feeling the silver and copper coins chink as you put them in your pocket. It gives worth to what you do because it has such a tangible result.

Once a month or perhaps it was every week we got a 'bonus'. This was usually in the form of a pack or packs of cheap cigarettes. As I didn't smoke I gave mine away to one of the others. Everyone looked forward to the bonus, though once there was what at Singleton & Cole's amounted to a workers' rebellion when Fred gave us each a packet of 'self-lighting cigarettes'. This was stock the company couldn't shift and when we got to work the following Monday I understood why. The cigarettes were tipped with something resembling match phosphorous which you struck against the side of the packet to ignite. 'No matches, no lighters. Brilliant!' the manufacturers must have thought. The trouble was at the first drag your lungs filled with smoke from the phosphorous which by all accounts smelled and tasted horrible. Fred was surrounded by complaining assemblers and checkers who returned the 'self-lighters' and refused to accept them as a bonus. Fred relayed this to the managers who relented and instructed him to hand out Park Drive or some other cheap brand instead. A crisis in management-worker relations had been averted and it never happened again while I was there.

I liked the people at Singleton and Cole's. When I left at the end of the summer of 1966 they gave me a book token, from 'Pauline, Lil, Sandra, Mary, C. Mary, Steve, Anne, Steff, Pam, Frank, Fred, Alan, Dennis, Ken, Wishing you every success in the future from all your friends at S&C.' I stuck the card into the book I bought, *La justicia de enero* by Sergio Galindo.

Monica

'About this time Monica and I began to drift apart.' That sounds convincing. It is the kind of acceptable explanation you tell yourself. The truth is I was doing the drifting. When I returned to Birmingham in the autumn of 1964, Monica got her first teaching job at a school in Cirencester. Our letters became less frequent, and eventually they stopped.

Some people have a remarkably clear idea of what they want in life. Monica, I believe, wanted to marry and have children, live a life centred on home and profession. We discussed the future now and then. Monica knew it would begin with a white wedding in St Mary's, Canon Davies officiating. There would be bridesmaids, a reception, and a honeymoon.

I sometimes tried to imagine it. There I would be, stiff and awkward in a new suit, the best man, probably my brother, at my side; the Vicar before me, beetle-browed; the organ, its base rumbling while the organist executed curlicues in the treble; anxiety about the ring, my brother patting his pocket; the pews crowded with family and friends, the women dressed in unfamiliar pastels, heavy with make-up; outrageous hats as worn by the Queen; then a stirring, the organist breaking into 'Here Comes the Bride', and me turning to see Monica, veiled, escorted by her father with slicked down hair a bit like Dagwood Bumstead. Monica and I would stand side by side while we repeated the marriage vows; I would place the ring on her finger; then I would lift the veil, look into her eyes and we would kiss.

My mother would have loved it, but I couldn't see myself in this scenario. This was part of the Old

Abergavenny I had rebelled against and was breaking loose from. I didn't believe in God, or the Church, or in Marriage. Even now I find the peel of church bells oppressive — *Dee-dee-dee-dee-daa-daa-daa-dum. Dee-dee-dee-dee-daa-daa-daa-dum* — ringing me back into the past.

I spent Christmas 1964 in Nürnberg, my first Christmas away from home. I had been invited by Reinhard who was now married himself. He had sent me wedding photographs — a church wedding of the kind Monica and my mother dreamed of. There was Reinhard, in formal dress with a white bow tie emerging with his bride from the church, there they were cutting the cake. He and his wife Hildegard now lived in a suburban house. Reinhard taught English and French in a gymnasium outside Nürnberg, Hildegard taught domestic science in the city. Children were soon on the way. Reinhard, too, seemed to know what he wanted out of life.

After Christmas it was arranged we would go for a few days skiing in the Austrian Alps together with one of Reinhard's brothers and his friend Werner. I had never skied and Reinhard loaned me an old pair of skis which, unfortunately as it turned out, had bindings that were fixed, rather than the modern kind that unlock if you have an accident.

I was no skier. I struggled to keep my balance even on a gentle slope, while children of four and five whizzed past encouraged by their parents. Sometimes I stood at the side of the advanced slopes and watched in admiration as young men, ski sticks tucked under their arms, crouched and fled downhill at incredible speeds over the hissing ice, only to slide to an elegant halt at the bottom.

Then I returned to my stumbling attempts on the nursery slope while Reinhard and the others trudged off to find something more challenging.

It happened on the last afternoon. The sun was already setting and I thought I'd make one last attempt at not falling over. Perhaps the sun had melted the surface of the snow making it more treacherous, but soon I was going faster than usual, then out of control, tumbling over in a confusion of sticks and skis. I heard, rather than felt, a snap in my left ankle like the snap of a chicken wishbone and even though there was no pain I knew I had broken something.

When I disentangled myself from the skis I tried to get up but couldn't put any weight on my left leg. I had somehow to get back to the Gasthaus, so I called to two skiers who were making their way back up the slope and tried to explain in pigeon-German. They understood, and one of them went to get help while the other stayed with me. Eventually two men appeared with a kind of sledge-stretcher and I was hauled and skied back to the Gasthaus. It was dark by then and impossible to get me down the mountain. I spent the evening in the bar, my leg on a stool, the ankle swelling and swelling until I had to untie the laces of my boot.

Next morning, the same two young men packed me onto the stretcher, covered me with a blanket and strapped me in. The stretcher, which was perhaps made of aluminium had shallow curved sides and a pair of long handles at either end. The journey to the valley below must have been at least three thousand feet down the side of the mountain along a narrow track through a forest of firs. Only then did I appreciate the joy of skiing, as we swung from side to side, the men hauling the sledge around, ice and snow hissing beneath us and flashing up to sting my cheeks. It was exhilarating watching the grey snow-laden sky and the boles of the trees flash past as we descended at speed. I had complete faith in my unknown companions and gave myself up entirely to the experience.

On the way to Germany I caught the train at Abergavenny and a postman of my acquaintance, Brian Pothecary, happened to be at the station collecting the mail. I had a duffle coat and a rucksack. 'Where are you going, then?' he asked. I explained. 'Ha-ha! You'll come back with your leg in plaster.'

In Nürnberg I went to a doctor who took an X-ray then encased my left leg in a plaster cast from the toes to the top of my thigh; I had broken a bone in my ankle. I borrowed a pair of crutches from him which I later returned by post and started on the long journey home by train across Germany. There was a storm in the Channel and on the ferry crossing I began to feel sick. This left me with a dilemma as it was impossible to crutch my way quickly enough in the crowded ship to the toilets. I decided that fresh air might do some good, so I went out onto the port gangway and stood propped against the wall of the saloon, rucksack on my back, taking deep breaths of wonderfully cold air. It worked, though I was tried by people on the upper deck leaning over the side and throwing up, threads of vomit whipping past to disappear in the wind and dark.

When I got back to Abergavenny it was my bad luck to find Brian at the station again loading mailbags onto a porter's flatbed trolley. 'Ha-ha — told you so!' he said as I crutched my way over the bridge.

Because of the difficulty of making my way around Birmingham by bus on a pair of crutches, it was agreed that I could work at home, the University Library sending me books by post. I was in plaster for about two months and when the cast was finally cut away I naively expected to be able to get up and carry on as normal, but the muscles had atrophied in the lower leg and when I put my foot down it flopped over as if made of jelly. Only after several weeks of physiotherapy was I able to walk properly again.

During this time, Monica came to the house. Perhaps it was half-term at her school. To my amazement — because learning to drive was one step too far in my world — she now had a moped and had driven all the way from Cirencester. We talked in the front room where we had sat so often over the past six years and Monica told me that one of her colleagues was courting her and that they were engaged. She said when she went to tell her relations in Abergavenny, they assumed it was me.

Eventually she got up to leave and I followed her out to the side door on Priory Road. There was her brand new moped. The machine somehow symbolised the distance between us — she had grown up and entered the adult world, and that was the last thing I wanted to do. She put on a helmet that made her face seem unfamiliar, smiled and drove off down Hereford Road. Not long after her marriage, my mother wrote to me in Copenhagen to say that Monica had visited our house with her new baby daughter. That was the last I ever heard of her.

The Shakespeare Institute

When I knew it in the 1960s, the Shakespeare Institute was housed at Westmere, a Victorian mansion in leafy Edgbaston Park Road. The house had been secured for English by T.J.B. Spencer against stiff opposition from other departments, or so I understood. 'You never know what's brewing in that Devil's Kitchen of a mind of his,' Rodney Hilton, Professor of Medieval History, had been heard to mutter. Almost every time he came to the Institute for one of the postgraduate medieval seminars he held with Geoffrey Shepherd, Rodney couldn't resist looking around and making a sarcastic comment.

There couldn't have been a better working environment for a postgraduate. The first floor was almost entirely taken up with an extensive library, mostly relating to Shakespeare and the Renaissance, with tables scattered about where you could read and write. There was a typing room, too, with a dozen or so typewriters. On the second floor there was a warren of smaller rooms that would have been the servants' bedrooms; these were mostly occupied by postgraduates as semi-official studies.

On the ground floor the rooms were oak-panelled. As you came in through the front door there was a reception area and then a lounge where we could chat and drink coffee or read the newspapers that were delivered every day. Beyond was Professor Spencer's room. Terence was a tall, well built man, but he seemed to have a head that was too large for his body. His pace when he walked was a kind of leaning-forward gallop. If we were still reading the morning papers when he arrived, he would say something like 'Good morning, gentlemen' as he passed briskly through carrying what looked like a heavy briefcase. If he was in a bad mood, he said nothing. Terence had the gift of headmasters and other wielders of power of making you feel ill-at-ease, something I never felt with Geoffrey Shepherd or Rodney Hilton. We went on reading for a few minutes for form's sake, then folded the newspapers and went off to our desks.

Westmere stood in its own grounds, with a croquet lawn, several other lawns and extensive flowerbeds looked after by a full-time gardener. The lawns led down to a wood surrounding a lake, beyond which were the fairways of Edgbaston Golf Club. It was easy to forget you were in the middle of a city.

The Institute, as its name implied, was a research centre for Shakespeare and Renaissance studies, but of the twenty or so postgraduates, three or four of us were medievalists. We were left to ourselves except that like the Renaissance postgraduates we were expected to attend Thursday afternoon seminars. These were a nightmare for me because the discussion usually centred on a play by Shakespeare or one of the Elizabethan or Jacobean dramatists about whom I knew very little. Chairs would be placed in a double semi-circle in the large seminar room that looked out to the croquet lawn in one direction and to the wood in another. Facing the semi-circle was a chair for Professor Spencer. At 2.30 we gathered and I picked a chair in the back row as far out of sight as possible. Apart from us postgraduates there would be research fellows and lecturers from the English Department such as Stanley Wells.

A seminar might begin with someone giving a short paper, or Professor Spencer might simply ask a question meant to provoke discussion. The trouble was it rarely did and he would then go round the two semi-circles asking each of us in turn what we thought. 'Mr Smallwood, lead us off...' 'Mr Walker...' 'Mr Donovan, enlighten us...' The first semi-circle done he would turn to the second, each person ticked off like seconds on the Clock of Doom until he came to me. 'Mr Barnie...' I usually responded with something pathetic like 'Well, I agree with So-and-So', and once or twice admitted that I had nothing to say. It was always a humiliation and when the seminar eventually ended I left the room in a cold sweat.

If a visiting lecturer gave a paper we were let off the hook because Spencer, in the chair, merely opened up discussion to questions from the floor. These were mostly dull affairs but once, in 1966 or '67, a young Stanley Fish gave a talk on Milton which got up the collective nose of the Renaissance specialists. When he finished there was silence until Spencer got himself together and said, 'Well! I'm sure that will send reverberations through the Institute for weeks.' The discussion afterwards was animated with the normally mild-mannered Elsie Duncan-Jones leaning forward at one point to shout, 'I will never believe you! *Never!*'

Terence Spencer was the model of a certain kind of urbanity which I never came across when I grew up in Abergavenny. It is the urbanity of Conservative politicians and Oxbridge dons, a charmed circle from which others are excluded by accent and demeanour. It is an urbanity by means of which men speak to men within the conventions of 'good form'. I have never been able to deal with this. It makes me defensive, wary, unwilling to reveal myself. I have never been a man among men in their sense because they present me with a mirror in which I see myself as the Abergavenny shopkeeper's boy, no better than I should be. I never had this experience when I lived in Denmark and I have never had it in Wales, but among the educated English middle class I feel as my father would have done, false-footed and inferior.

Sometime after I moved back to Abergavenny in 1982 my wife Helle and I were invited to the fiftieth birthday dinner of a friend of ours. He and his wife were ceramicists and apart from their two teenage boys the only other guest was an art critic who wrote for *The Times*. He was very formal in a suit while the rest of us were casually dressed. He had the kind of English urbanity I'm talking about, though with a waspish edge. He told us he had recently moved to one of the small English border towns north of Hereford. I said, 'Oh, I like —' to which he replied that it was terribly dull and provincial.

The conversation drifted here and there, amicably enough, but then the critic raised the question of the difference between art and poetry, and something strange happened. Art, he said, truly was an art. It took years to learn the craft, on top of which you had to be inspired. Poetry, on the other hand, could be written by anyone; it took no skill. Everyone around the table demurred, but yes, he insisted, even five-year-olds could do it. I suggested that five-year-olds could also do paintings, but, no, that was completely wrong. I asked if he thought anyone could have written *The Waste Land*. Yes, of course. The others joined in, but we went round in circles, always returning to his flat statement that poetry was nothing, anyone could write it at the drop of a hat.

I think, looking back, my friends must have told him I was a poet by way of introduction before we arrived and that he had taken a dislike to me for some reason and wanted to goad me. It is difficult otherwise to explain why he started such a ridiculous conversational hare. Perhaps he thought I was dull and provincial like the people in his adopted border town. It didn't matter from what angle any of us approached the subject, he remained suave and ironic — poetry was child's play.

I shouldn't have, but eventually I lost my temper. It was a mistake because such a man never loses his. He had won his little game and short of getting up and hitting him there was nothing to do but leave. I heard later the others carried on arguing with him long after we had gone even though there was no point. The man was either malicious or a fool, and I knew which I thought he was.

Years later when I was editor of *Planet*, I went to a reception at the Institute of Contemporary Arts in London, organised by the Books Council in yet another futile attempt to get the London media interested in Welsh literature. As we stood with glasses of wine the publicity agent who had organised it came up and asked me who I would like to meet. Looking around at the men in suits and the well-dressed women I didn't want to meet anyone, but I couldn't say that, so hoping he wasn't there, I said 'Oh, what about the editor of the *TLS*?' Unfortunately he *was* there, standing in the middle of the room talking to one of his kind. I was introduced as the editor of *Planet*. He and his companion looked at me, asked a question or two, then turned to each other and picked up the thread of their conversation. Dismissed, I went across to a knot of Welsh people and talked with them for the rest of the evening.

I only saw Terence Spencer's mask slip once. There was a middle-aged Italian scholar at the

Institute for a while, a rather strange man with cropped sandy hair and steel-rimmed glasses. He wore black detachable sleeves, elasticated at either end, which he slipped over the shirt sleeves on his forearms when he was working, rather like a clerk in a Victorian counting house.

One day as I was coming back from lunch at the refectory I heard a scuffle behind the front door of Westmere and out came Terence, bundling the Italian before him and propelling him down the steps. 'Go!' he shouted, raising an arm. 'Go! And never come back!' 'I will getta the law on you,' the Italian shouted as Terence slammed the door. Nobody seemed to know what the row was about but we never saw the Italian again.

How Canada Changed My Life

As a postgraduate I started going to the University Film Society which showed a film once a month in the Chemistry Department in the old part of the University. This took place in a large lecture hall with steeply banked tiers of benches and you got there early to make sure of a good seat in the middle.

Whoever was on the committee had taste, and in my five years at the Shakespeare Institute I gained an education in the history of film, from D.W. Griffith's *Birth of a Nation*, Eisenstein's *Ivan the Terrible* and *Battleship Potemkin* to the great silent comedies of Buster Keaton and Charlie Chaplin, and on through classic Westerns, *film noir*, Italian and French film of the 1950s and '60s and the major films of Ingmar Bergman, many of them as they came out. Then there was the new wave of British film — especially, for me, Joseph Losey's *The Servant*, *Blow Up* and *Accident*. I absorbed them all, except Chaplin who I never liked for his sugary appeal to the pathetic and the sentimental. Keaton's deadpan in films like *The General* was and is more to my taste.

Of them all it was Bergman I was most taken with — the sombre stoicism and tragic view of life of *The Seventh Seal* and *Virgin Spring*, the confrontation of despair in *Winter Light* and *The Silence*; the lyricism and gentle humour of *Wild Strawberries*. Years later when I read his memoirs, diary, fiction and scripts in Swedish, his importance for me grew. Together with the poetry and fiction of Harry Martinson and the novels of Joseph Conrad, Bergman became a cornerstone of the view of life I was working toward in the 1960s.

Film Society audiences were a mixed bunch of students from the humanities and sciences who were usually well behaved and often knowledgeable. We disgraced ourselves only once at a screening of *The Cabinet of Dr Caligari*, the German horror film from 1920. Hardly anyone liked its highly stylised scenery and grotesquely exaggerated acting and after about fifteen minutes there was unrest on the back benches with a lot of laughing and joking. A woman below us in one of the front rows eventually stood up and turned round. She had a horsey face with hair pulled severely back in a pony tail. '*Philistines!*' she shouted. This was a mistake given the general mood of mockery we had fallen into. Soon paper darts were whizzing toward her from the back benches.

One of the students at the Shakespeare Institute was B—. She had been a couple of years below me as an undergraduate and I had not known her then. Now she was doing an MA in Renaissance studies. I saw her around and we talked occasionally. She had long honey-blonde hair which cascaded down to her waist, and a beautiful dreamy smile. One evening early in the summer of 1966 I was walking back from the Film Society with some friends on the way to the Gun Barrels. B— was walking by herself in front of us and the thought came into my head, 'I'm in love with her.' We overtook her and she joined us for a drink. From that moment I started courting her.

Ours was a strange relationship. I think our feelings for each other were mutual, but as I discovered, something had happened which made her reluctant to commit herself wholly to anyone in the few months I knew her. We became very close but it was a closeness that was only ever sealed with a kiss. There was no time. B— had won a scholarship to study in Canada and was due to sail from Liverpool at the end of August.

With my own MA coming to an end I approached Geoffrey Shepherd about the possibility of doing a PhD with him. One of Geoffrey's distinguishing features was a mind that was speculative, ranging widely across many fields. He wasn't an historian himself but while I was talking with him in his office he remarked in passing that someone ought to look at the literature of the fourteenth and fifteenth centuries to see how it reflected the Hundred Years War. This appealed to me and when he agreed to take me on I suggested this as a topic for research.

My Lower Second meant I had no chance of a state grant, but Birmingham had a small number of research grants of its own reserved for graduates of the University. Despite my lack of ease in the presence of Terence Spencer I will always be grateful to him for putting my name forward. Eventually I heard I was first on the reserve list and that everything depended on a woman finishing an MA in Canada. She had yet to accept the offer of a grant from Birmingham.

After a few tense weeks I heard in August that the woman wasn't coming back and that the one-year grant was mine. I discussed this with B——. I couldn't bear the thought of losing her and suggested I abandon the PhD and follow her to Canada where I could surely find some kind of job — after all, I had worked on the post and the buses and in a warehouse. B— however wouldn't agree. Our feelings for each other had developed so suddenly and we had only known each other a few months. I think also that she saw Canada as the future — a new beginning that didn't involve what had happened to her, or anyone from her past, including me.

The summer of 1966 was warm and sunny. One Friday B— and I took the train to Abergavenny for a weekend. We climbed the Sugar Loaf and lay in the heather on its slopes amid the hum of insects. The week before she left I saw her every day. She said she would write from Canada but I knew our relationship was ending. On the last day we walked down Edgbaston Park Road toward the Institute and half way we stopped and kissed.

I went to Abergavenny and when I knew she would be sailing put some blues on the record player and drank my way through a bottle of sherry. It did me no good and gave me a vile hangover. A day or so later I returned to the Shakespeare Institute with its capacious rooms and gardens and leafy wood to carry on without her.

Berlin

In the summer of 1967 I visited Reinhard in Nürnberg again and from there we went by train to Berlin. I didn't much like West Berlin. It had a frenzied, neurotic edge, especially at night when the streets blazed with neon. We visited a crowded late-night bar that had banks of TV monitors, each showing a different loop of film, a chaos of images watched by drinkers with indifference. Disco music drowned out any attempt at conversation. This was the West's showcase, febrile, vulgar, marooned within a grim communist state.

One evening we ascended a tall building to an observation point on the roof. Below was West Berlin, a galaxy ablaze. But move round to the other side and there was East Berlin, a black void, a light shining weakly here and there, a non-existence.

Perhaps it was next morning we crossed the border for the day. As a British passport holder I had to cross at Checkpoint Charlie, while Reinhard, his brother and Werner crossed at a checkpoint reserved for West Germans. Waved through by the Americans I was scrutinised by the East Berlin border guards and had to have the amount of East German marks in my possession registered before I was let through.

The checkpoint for West Germans must have been quite close because I know we met up quickly and took a walk through the city centre. Instantly I felt this was a Berlin I knew, but a Berlin from the war and my childhood. We walked across a vast, empty square; there was a cathedral still in ruins from allied bombing or the Russian bombardment, its cupola shattered. Everywhere façades were pockmarked by shrapnel or bullets. The sky was grey and it had been raining, and grey seemed the colour of East Berlin. We watched the changing of the guard outside a government building, the soldiers goose-stepping, their boots banged down hard on the paving slabs.

My cousin John Hodges had been here in 1945 as an officer in either the military police or the intelligence services. In 1939 he was studying French in Paris with Margaret his future wife. By climbing over barriers at the Gare du Nord they caught the last train to Calais and England before the Germans arrived — according to my mother. Six years later he was in the ruins of Berlin with the British army. In my mother's story he was walking down a bomb-damaged street one day when he saw a portrait of himself on display in the window of a photographer's shop. It was the only portrait in the window. He went in and had it removed. My mother claimed he was involved in hunting down Nazis and the photograph was a warning to others from a Nazi sympathiser. I only met John once or twice and have no idea if the story is true. Coming from my mother's lips it would certainly have to be questionable. It is possible, I suppose, that my cousin was involved in the denazification process in some way.

John I imagine is dead and I will never know the truth, but the story has a haunting quality that has remained with me — my cousin, an Abergavenny boy, coming face to face with himself in a photographer's window, and me twenty-two years later walking the same streets that were still marked by the catastrophe of war; streets Radomir would have been familiar with too when he was there at the same time interpreting for the British.

We took an evening meal in the Opera House Café. It was as if we had stumbled into the 1920s. There were palms in pots dotted about; waiters in old-fashioned formal dress with bow ties; stiff linen tablecloths and napkins; and a trio playing café music of half a century before. The place was devoid of customers. I forget what we ate, I only remember this atmosphere of displacement in time and a feeling that either they or we were unreal, the work of someone's imagination.

Afterwards we made our way back to the checkpoints It was dark with only a dim street light here and there. There were one or two cars and no pedestrians as we walked down cobbled side streets. We split up at last and I made my way to Checkpoint Charlie. I passed a ground floor window in a narrow street that had a poster of a passenger jet soaring into a blue sky. 'Fly KLM to Canada', it said in German. I wondered who put it there and how such an ironic display had not been removed by the authorities.

Years earlier during the war my wife's uncle, Jørgen Jensen, had flown to Berlin on a regular basis. He was a navigator with the Danish airline DDL (Det Danske Luftfartsselskab) and his brother Poul was a pilot. With Poul's future wife Hanne as air hostess they made the weekly flight from Malmö in southern Sweden via Copenhagen to Berlin and back. I had heard about this in a general way but it was well known in the family that Jørgen never talked about his wartime experience and I only met Poul, who lived in Stockholm, a few times.

Then at a family dinner a few years ago when he was in his eighties, Jørgen started to reminisce, almost as if talking to himself. They had flown Junkers JU52s, he recalled, those state-of-the-art German passenger planes of the late 1930s that had a third engine in the nose. Their passengers had been a mix of Swedish and Danish businessmen travelling to Berlin to negotiate deals, Nazi officials from occupied Denmark, and Wehrmacht and SS officers going to and fro on leave. There was a regular routine — take off from Malmö, pick up passengers in Copenhagen, then direct to Tempelhof where they stayed overnight in a hotel before returning next day.

One day, perhaps late in the war, Jørgen and Poul were approached in Malmö by a man who said he was from the British consulate. Would they spy on troop movements, he wanted to know, as they flew across Germany. The brothers agreed and there began an intense period in their lives. Jørgen as navigator made a note of the co-ordinates of large masses of troops and armour as they flew overhead and these were passed on to the consulate when they returned to Malmö. Jørgen would have been twenty-two or twenty-three at the time, his brother a few years older.

The information was then handed to military intelligence in London and used by the RAF to bomb and strafe the German units Jørgen had identified. Sitting at the table after the dishes had been cleared and bent with age he recalled how terrible he felt in the knowledge that information he provided would lead to the deaths perhaps of hundreds of men he had seen remotely from the air. Only destruction of the Nazi armies could have brought the war to an end, and Jørgen whose country was occupied, would have known this, but he was a gentle, quietly-spoken man and it was easy to understand his anguish.

Amazingly, the flights continued into the final weeks of the war. Jørgen said that toward the end, on approaching and taking off from Tempelhof they flew as low as they could to avoid Russian fighter planes, but the routine remained the same —

overnight at a Berlin hotel then back to Copenhagen and Malmö. On one of the very last flights out of Tempelhof they could see the battle raging on the outskirts of the city, plumes of smoke and soundless explosions. As they rose, the wings began to ice up and the ice on the leading edge was black from the smoke of the battle.

In the end Jørgen's wife received a phone call warning her to get word to them not to return to Copenhagen because the Gestapo were about to arrest them. So the brothers stayed in Sweden and waited out the last terrible weeks of the war while Berlin was destroyed.

Outside, while Jørgen was telling us this, it was an ordinary summer day in a north Copenhagen suburb. A hundred yards across the main road were the narrow reaches of the Sound and beyond the low coastline of Sweden.

Book Raids

At the Shakespeare Institute there was a small group of us who collected books. Catalogues from second-hand and antiquarian dealers came through the post all the time and we scoured them for books in our subject areas. Best of all we went on book raids. One or two of the postgraduates owned cars and depending on the car's capacity, four or five of us would pile in and drive to Worcester, Leodbury, Hereford, and Hay-on-Wye, taking in every second-hand bookshop on the way; or drive toward Oxford ending up at Thornton's in Broad Street. Today of course you would probably go on the net. I have certainly picked up rare books in this way from as far afield as San Francisco and Queensland that I never would have found in a hundred years of browsing in shops within my geographical reach.

There is nonetheless the excitement of the chase which can only be had in the presence of thousands of books in a shop, higgledy-piggledy or ordered on shelves, piled high on staircases and floors. Most may be of no interest but then a book stands out and you grasp it. In this way I obtained a translation of Richard de Bury's *The Love of Books* and assembled a complete set of medieval English chronicles in Bohn's Antiquarian Library. Then there are the leather-bound editions of Young's *Night Thoughts* and Somerville's *The Chace*. *Night Thoughts*, I see, cost me 35s in an edition of 1773 which was at the top end of what I could afford then. I had never heard of Somerville or *The Chace*, which is a celebration of hunting in blank verse, until Terence Spencer came into the institute one day enthusing about it. He read some passages to us that stayed in my mind and on one of our raids I came across it in an edition from 1767 which I could afford.

Much later, in Copenhagen, I picked up a first edition of *Aniara* signed by Harry Martinson for 500kr. Most people don't mind in what edition they read a book which is why e-readers will probably conquer the world. Ned Thomas was sitting next to an American couple on a plane once. The man was reading a paperback and as he finished a page he tore it out and gave it to his wife. You can be sure they have long since gone over to Kindles. But a well-crafted book is deeply satisfying in a way that a text composed of pixels on a screen can never be. With older books, too, there is the patina given them by time — the intricate gilt scrolls on the leather binding of my copy of *Night Thoughts*, for example; or the iconography of the books published by several of H.M. Stanley's officers in their dispute with him over the failure of the Emin Pasha Relief Expedition. The very design of these books is integral to their meaning in a way that is lost in a modern edition.

I have Joseph Conrad's *Notes on My Books*, too, in a limited edition of 250 signed copies published in 1921 three years before he died. My copy is No. 11, signed with Conrad's distinctive flourish in blue ink. There is another book signed by Martinson — a first edition of *Cikada* from 1953 with the inscription 'Till Andreas från Harry med vänskap' (To Andreas from Harry in friendship). Martinson and Conrad have had the greatest influence on my ideas about writing and about the human condition. To have these copies brings me closer to them in a way which I acknowledge is not rational but which is meaningful all the same. I regret never asking R.S. Thomas to sign his books for me. He always seemed severe about such things though I know he did sign books for others. He too influenced me over many years, firstly in his portrayal of rural mid Wales which was not so distant from my own Black Mountains, but more significantly, I now think, in his versification. Thomas himself had learned from William Carlos Williams as he once admitted (to my surprise) when I asked him about it in an interview. Especially after *H'm*, R.S. was a master of free verse in which line breaks are used to conduct the rhythm of a poem against the expectations of syntax, drawing the reader's eye and mind across fractured lines to the conclusion. I find this kind of rhythmic counterpointing exciting and I learned a great deal from him, and from Williams and A.R. Ammons.

Some of the books I remember are the ones that got away, like volume 1 of the first edition of *Biographia Literaria* which I found on one of the raids. It was cheap and I could easily have afforded it, but then I thought what's the point of an odd volume. I remember the binding, the title page, and the beautiful clarity of the print; I have never seen a copy since.

I suppose on these trips we must have eaten lunch — a pie and a pint most likely — but then it was back to the car, or on occasion two cars, and on the road to the next small town and its second-hand bookshop. None of us had much money though my Birmingham University research grant of £500 seemed a fortune to me then. We lived cheaply and apart from food and beer at the Gun Barrels all our money went on books.

We got back to the Shakespeare Institute in the evening, the car nosing down into the drive, feeling good after a day sifting through stock in a dozen dusty shops, the boot of the car weighed down with our finds.

The Dream of Being a Scholar

One of the books I read at this time was E.R. Curtius's *European Literature and the Latin Middle Ages*. Curtius had an extraordinarily wide ranging mind that spanned European literary culture from Homer to Goethe and beyond — he was the first to translate *The Waste Land* into German and wrote perceptively about James Joyce. The book was written amid the ruins of Europe after the Second World War and was an argument and a plea for the unity of European culture despite the catastrophes of the twentieth century.

I learned a great deal from it, as I did from Geoffrey Shepherd who had a similar mind. Geoffrey was familiar with European literature in several languages. His field was nominally the Middle Ages and early Renaissance but his horizons went far beyond.

On one occasion we were discussing the Romantics when I disparaged Robert Southey in comparison with Wordsworth and Coleridge. Geoffrey pulled down a battered collection of Southey's poetry and read from one of his long — and still to my mind dreary — historical poems. I noticed that the pages were covered with annotations in his minuscule handwriting. He pointed out how well read Southey was and how his reading informed the footnotes he appended to his poems. He also said that Southey had a family to maintain from his writing and that, unlike Coleridge, he was a man who lived by a sense of duty to those who depended on him. Geoffrey was a high Anglican whose position was very similar in many ways to that of T.S. Eliot, and a sense of duty was at the centre of his being. I have no doubt that an event in Copenhagen shortly after I had gone there would have caused him to think I had failed in mine.

Years later when I taught the Romantics for the Open University in Cardiff I came to understand what Shepherd was saying. Southey is not a great poet but his poetry should be seen in the light of the kind of man he was and the struggle he endured. Before you can judge you have to understand. When he became senile, Southey wandered about his library looking at his books, taking one down but too far gone to be able to read.

Geoffrey had read Ted Hughes, too, at a time when he was only a name to me. I wanted to have that range, that ease of access to European literary culture. At the time I was reading novelists like Pío Baroja and Camilo José Cela in Spanish with the aid of a dictionary. For my research I had to get up Medieval Latin, Anglo-Norman and Old French to read Froissart and Christine de Pisan, John Gower's Latin and Anglo-Norman poetry, the parliamentary rolls and the chronicles. I may even have read one or two books that Geoffrey hadn't, like the Latin sermons of Bishop Brinton, though I would not have been surprised had he pulled down an annotated copy from his shelves. A few of us at the Shakespeare Institute also attended seminars given by Terence Spencer in which we read *The Aeneid* and *The Divine Comedy* in the original, and another seminar with Shepherd in which we read through some of the texts in E.V. Gordon's *An Introduction to Old Norse*.

Some of this was abortive. I stuck with Old Norse because I was fascinated by the literature and read a number of the family sagas and the Greenland sagas in Old Icelandic, but *The Aeneid* was beyond me, the syntax too complex and unfamiliar so that I struggled for hours to translate and understand even a couple of lines. I gave up on *The Divine Comedy* too. Dante's malicious pleasure in the punishments of the damned revolted me. I had caught the tail end of all that in Abergavenny and I wanted no more. It didn't matter how great the poetry was supposed to be.

This was not a good start. If I was trying to follow in the footsteps of Curtius and Shepherd it might be said I had already lost them in the woods. The truth is I was never a scholar though it took me a long time to admit this to myself. My PhD thesis was good enough for Rodney Hilton to recommend it to Weidenfeld and Nicolson with whom he had connections, and after I had rewritten it for publication it appeared as *War in Medieval Society* in 1974. With a slightly different title it was co-published by Cornell University Press in America. I was proud of it then but I cannot even read a paragraph of it now. It is ironic therefore that it is the only book of mine which has ever sold out.

I knew of course that my grasp of Medieval Latin and Anglo-Norman was slender, but so was my knowledge of Middle English which it really ought not to have been. In one of the postgraduate seminars run by Hilton and Shepherd we were discussing the alliterative poem *Winnere and Wastour*. Geoffrey knew that I had just been reading it for my research so when discussion turned to a particular passage which Rodney and the history postgraduates couldn't understand, he asked me to translate. But I only read this kind of poetry by constant reference to the glossary and in the seminar of course there was no time for that. I made a poor show of it, and when Geoffrey had to take over I could sense his annoyance.

At Copenhagen University where Old and Middle English texts were only taught as sources for historical linguistics, I taught them as literature. I enjoyed teaching *Beowulf, The Battle of Maldon*, Chaucer, and *Sir Gawain and the Green Knight* in this way, but often the students' grasp of grammar was better than mine and I had to do an immense amount of work to disguise this. From the beginning I had always responded to the poetry and it never mattered to me if I missed a word or had to keep turning to the glossary. It was the emotional power of the poetry that counted:

Þe fayre hede fro þe halce hit to þe erþe,
Þat fele hit foyned with her fete, pere hit forth roled;
Þe blod brayd fro þe body, þat blykked on þe grene;
And nawper faltered ne fel þe freke neuer þe helder,
Bot styply he start forth vpon styf schonkes,
And runyschly he raght out, pere as renkkez stoden,
Laght to his lufly hed, and lyft hit vp sone...

Despite these shortcomings I still thought of myself as a scholar and when my thesis was finished in 1971 I looked about for another project. In my reading of the Latin chronicles I had noticed that descriptions of kings and queens, lords and prelates, tended to conform to a pattern. There might be personal observation in them if a chronicler was close to the court, or there might be genuine detail gleaned at second or third hand, but this appeared within a stylised matrix that had its origins, I suspected, in medieval teaching on rhetoric, derived ultimately of course from Classical Roman rhetorical treatises. So I began reading some of the handbooks from the Middle Ages, then moved back to their sources in texts like the *Rhetorica ad Herennium* before moving outward to Cicero and Quintilian to get a broader view of the Classical rhetorical tradition. These I read in English in the Loeb Classics, glancing now and then across at the Latin. At the same time I was rereading the chronicles.

I did this for two or three years, making copious notes, but gradually my interest began to flag and I became more and more reluctant to open one of the bright red Loebs that I had collected so assiduously.

Then one night I had a dream in which a short poem wrote itself in my head. I woke up and felt impelled to write it down. I left the biro and piece of paper by the bedside and went back to sleep. I don't know how long afterwards it was, but I dreamed another poem, woke up and wrote that down too. When I got up next morning I knew that what I wanted to do was write poems. I abandoned the study of rhetoric and the Latin chronicles and began instead to read as widely as I could in British and American poetry from the Modernists on. I had begun teaching myself Welsh at this time and started to read a few poets like Gwenallt and Waldo Williams, as well as widening my reading of Welsh poetry in English beyond R.S. Thomas and Dylan Thomas.

The Engelsk Institut at Copenhagen University was a very liberal place for teachers in the 1970s, and after a couple of years of intensive reading I abandoned medieval studies and taught twentieth-century English and American poetry instead, as well as courses on the blues in the American Studies programme, and together with Irish and Scots colleagues a joint course on 'Anglo-Celtic' literature and culture.

Were the previous ten years a waste? It is hard to say. If I had studied something else I would not have applied for a post at Copenhagen University, I would never have met Helle, or learned Danish, or read Harry Martinson in Swedish. Some dark things would also not have happened, or not have happened in the same way.

But there is no guarantee I would have started writing poetry earlier. The dreams were a dam bursting, but there had to be water in the dam first. It was to be ten years before I had a poetry pamphlet published and another three before my first book-length collection, by which time I was 46. That is late for a poet and it left me out of synch with my contemporaries in Wales. The probability, however, is that there is nothing I could have done differently

I have long ago mislaid the poems I dreamed and wrote down. I cannot even remember what they were about. Their function was to release me into a new, chancy world governed by the imagination.

1968

But that is to look to the future. In 1968 I was in the second year of my PhD and deep in the study of the Hundred Years War. That Easter, though, I took time out to meet Reinhard in Paris. We stayed in the rather luxurious flat of a French acquaintance of his who was away on holiday. It was very central and we were able to walk the streets to visit the Musée de Cluny and the Musée de l'Homme. We ate out rarely because of the expense but Reinhard had told me to bring my Student's Union card which enabled me to eat in the refectory at the Sorbonne. The food was at least different from what I was used to in Birmingham. As we moved along the queue at the self-service counter I saw what was described as 'lamb's tongue sandwich'. I thought that sounded interesting but when we sat down I found the description to be rather literal — a lamb's tongue stuck between two pieces of dry white bread with a bit of lettuce. The tongue looked as though it had just been plucked from the lamb's head and lightly boiled. I left it on the plate.

Once we visited a café famous for its onion soup in the old Les Halles. It was late in the evening and while we ate there was a commotion as police dragged two men away, one of them shouting 'Pays Basque libre! Pays Basque libre!' The door slammed shut behind them and everyone in the crowded café went on eating.

The most interesting event during our stay also involved the police. We were walking down a street when on turning a corner we saw forty or fifty policemen in riot gear, armed with batons and shields.

They stood at the end of the street facing a group of young men who jeered at them while grubbing up cobblestones to throw. We walked toward them curious as to what was going on when, without warning, the police charged, visors down and batons raised. It was a black wall of force against which the demonstrators were defenceless. There was panic and when the police were about ten paces from us we were pushed violently by the movement of the crowd through the door of a small restaurant, the diners looking up in alarm as the line of police rushed past. We had been lucky. The door of the restaurant opened inwards. Had it opened outwards we would have been trapped and no doubt had our heads knocked in and perhaps even been arrested as 'foreign student agitators'. It was the beginning of the '68 student revolution.

As a medievalist the encounter gave me an insight into what it must have been like to face an armed charge in war. These French police were unstoppable and they weren't even on horses. In the fourteenth century, three or four hundred heavily armoured knights charging on horseback would have been a terrifying sight even if by the mid fourteenth century the English had developed an effective counter-weapon in the form of the long bow — if the bowmen didn't cut and run.

Back in Birmingham I forgot about the incident until one evening in autumn when I was due to give a talk to a history research group. Their meetings were held in the staff lounge on the first floor of the Humanities building. I arrived on time but apart from Rodney Hilton and another member of the History Department no one else was present. The windows of the lounge looked out onto the green in front of the Library and I could see an unusual number of students milling about. When it was obvious no one else was going to show up Rodney suggested postponing the meeting. None of us was sure what was happening, but the animated knots of people standing on the green or running up and down the paths made it clear it was something out of the usual.

I can't remember if it was then or a few evenings later I attended a meeting on the green. The Library was approached by two sets of steps leading to a balustrade. With the Library as backdrop it was a suitable setting for a speech by Stalin or Lenin, and that is more or less what we got, for the student revolution I had seen in Paris had finally reached Birmingham. A group of 'revolutionaries' stood looking down on us over the balustrade. It was a cold evening and one of them who must have been short because we could only see his head, began to speak. 'Comrades,' the head said, 'thank you for coming. I know it's cold. You're cold, I'm cold.' 'Stand up, then,' someone shouted from the crowd, probably one of the electrical or mechanical engineers who I don't think took the revolution seriously.

I didn't take it seriously either, or rather I quickly decided to distance myself from it, after I witnessed some of the tactics of the Marxist students. I went to a meeting in the Great Hall which the students may or may not have occupied, I cannot now remember. The hall was crowded with a dais at the far end with a microphone and a PA system. It was supposed to be a debate, but every time someone went to the mike who opposed what was happening the sound was turned off. Then one of the Marxists would take over to harangue us. Members of the audience began to shout in protest and I started shouting too, unaware that one of the younger lecturers from the English Department had come in and was standing at my side. 'Hear him out,' he said, full of English fair play; but he hadn't been there when the 'revolutionaries' switched off the PA.

Even on the Continent, it seems to me now, the Marxists were naive. In Birmingham they were doubly so. In imitation of students at the Sorbonne who dreamed of forging a union between workers and intellectuals, the Birmingham revolutionaries sent delegates to building sites and factories around the city, only to be told to 'Eff off' by the hard-hats.

I had another encounter with the Marxists at Copenhagen University a couple of years later when I was co-opted onto a staff-student curriculum committee. There were four staff members and four students all of whom belonged to the Marxist political faction in the student body. They had been voted en bloc onto the committee because the majority of students weren't interested in spending long hours embroiled in university politics.

The meetings of the curriculum committee were time-consuming and tedious with endless arguments and any vote predictably ending in stalemate. Once or twice, partly because I didn't much like my colleagues on the committee, and partly because I occasionally thought the students had a point, I voted with them. We staff members were constantly breaking off for 'summemøde' (buzz meetings) to discuss tactics.

The students in Birmingham and Copenhagen were ideologues. They had absorbed a fashionable version of Marxism which absolved them from any need to think for themselves. Deep down they were conservative and authoritarian. It didn't surprise me years later to learn that one junior member of staff, an ardent Marxist, had become a Roman Catholic priest.

They were also ruthless. In Sweden in the early 1970s the Marxists inaugurated a witch hunt in the leftwing press against any writer held to be out of line. Harry Martinson, in particular, was attacked as a reactionary for daring to question the country's headlong rush into modernity. Today he is a prophet of the green movement, but in the '70s he was pilloried mercilessly. A sensitive man, he descended into a profound depression and was admitted to a psychiatric hospital in Stockholm. There in 1978 he committed hara-kiri with scissors.

Forty years ago the Marxists thought they were going to change the world. They did, but not in the way they intended. During the leftist upheaval of the late '60s and '70s conservatives kept their heads down; it was as if they no longer existed. In fact they were regrouping and at the end of the '70s they moved centre stage in the person of Margaret Thatcher and Ronald Reagan who instituted such a far-reaching revolution from the right that socialism has never recovered. The naive formulations of the Marxists bore no relation to the political and social power structures of the West but they opened the door to the world we live in today.

Joseph Conrad saw with great clarity the consequences of idealistic revolutions from the left when he made the English narrator of *Under Western Eyes* say to Nathalie Haldin:

...in a real revolution — not a simple dynastic change or a mere reform of institutions — in a real revolution the best characters do not come to the front. A violent revolution falls into the hands of narrow-minded fanatics and of tyrannical hypocrites at first. Afterwards comes the turn of the pretentious intellectual failures of the time. Such are the chiefs and the leaders. You will notice that I have left out the mere rogues. The

scrupulous and the just, the noble, human, and devoted natures;
the unselfish and the intelligent may begin a movement — but
it passes away from them. They are not the leaders of a
revolution. They are its victims: the victims of disgust, of
disenchantment — often of remorse. Hopes grotesquely
betrayed, ideals caricatured — that is the definition of
revolutionary success.

I witnessed this, in miniature, in Birmingham in 1968
and in Copenhagen in the early '70s.

Departure

By the autumn of 1968 I had one year left of my
state research grant and I knew I had to look for a
job. At the time, there were few posts in my field in
Britain and since I still had an interest in Old Norse
literature I wrote to the English Departments of the
Universities of Oslo, Stockholm, Uppsala, Lund and
Copenhagen asking if there were any vacancies. Most
replied in the negative but I received a scribbled note
from Professor Knud Schibsbye at Copenhagen
saying there was a one-year vacancy for a foreign
guest lecturer, would I like it?

I wrote an application and sent it with a CV to
the Professor. Weeks passed and I heard nothing so I
assumed I had not been successful. I wrote again to
be sure and received another hastily scribbled note
telling me, yes, I'd got the job, hadn't I realised? In
1969 professors still had certain university posts in
their gift.

The community of students from my time at the
Shakespeare Institute was breaking up. Several
Canadians all got university posts back in Canada, as
did three of the English postgraduates. One went to
South Africa, another to the University of
Strasbourg, and yet another to the University of
Malta. An American nun, plump and jolly, who always
dressed in bright civilian clothes, legged it over the
convent wall (so I heard) after returning to New
York.

Even the gardener retired that year. He kept to
himself in his shed, rolling his own, trundling a
wheelbarrow to the various flower beds. He never
seemed to strain himself but the garden and lawns

were always immaculate. There was a presentation for him in the lounge during which Professor Spencer gave an elegant, witty speech about gardeners in Shakespeare that must have gone straight over the old man's head. Everyone stood around busy not being embarrassed.

During this time I had been going out with Heather W— who was a student of Rodney Hilton's. Our relationship developed and when I knew I was going to Denmark I asked her if she would come with me. She agreed and we got married in Birmingham Registry Office in the summer of 1969.

I had no idea what to expect in Denmark, but I bought a copy of *Teach Yourself Danish* and a two-volume Danish-English/English-Danish dictionary, and began to learn the language. Danish grammar is comparatively straightforward for an English speaker, but Danish pronunciation is not. When I arrived in Copenhagen I discovered I had got it all wrong. Despite working hard at the grammar I couldn't distinguish word boundaries in speech and consequently couldn't understand a word that was said. I had to start all over again.

The autumn semester began in September so Heather and I decided to travel to Copenhagen at the beginning of August to find accommodation and settle in. We left Abergavenny by train, my mother crying on the platform as usual, and in London took the boat-train to Dover and the ferry to Oostende. From there we caught an express to Hamburg and then a sleeper to Copenhagen.

I slept little in the uncomfortable bunk bed and when the carriages were shunted rattling and clanking onto the ferry at Puttgarden I was wide awake. After crossing Fehmarn Bælt we docked at Rødby; the train was reassembled, and we sped across Lolland and

Falster. I got up and opened the curtains of our carriage window onto a brilliant summer morning, the light shining with what I came to think of as a special Scandinavian intensity. The train raced past endless fields of gold wheat beneath a luminous sky. It was impossible not to feel elated and that my first sight of Denmark was a good omen.

It was, however, to be the beginning of a dark period in both our lives caused solely by my hand. I cannot write about this, and so the mirror is turned to the wall.

It's Over

Be careful of that backward glance,
why after all would anyone return
to stony island and the cold stares
and the raised sticks and harpoons
of those you left behind; there are no

grass skirts or coloured shirts, just
bad ciné film that flicks and jumps,
and no one shouting 'Come on in,
the water's warm'; such fragments
are washed up mostly from the dead,

no pawnbroker would take them,
chips of glass and brick, and amber
smiles; walk out again under the doorbell's tinkle onto the street, shoulder
to shoulder with the passing crowd.